THE GREATEST FOOTBALL QUIZ BOOK

1,000 Questions on Football History,
Clubs and Players

THE GREATEST FOOTBALL QUIZ BOOK

1,000 Questions on Football History, Clubs and Players

Compiled by Chris Cowlin and Kevin Snelgrove

Foreword by Darren Anderton

APEX PUBLISHING LTD

First published in hardback in 2011 by

Apex Publishing Ltd

PO Box 7086, Clacton on Sea, Essex, CO15 5WN, England

www.apexpublishing.co.uk

British Library Cataloguing-in-Publication Data
A catalogue record for this book
is available from the British Library

ISBN: 1-906358-97-4   978-1-906358-97-6

Typeset in 10.5pt Chianti Bdlt Win95BT

Cover Design: Siobhan Smith

Printed and bound in Great Britain by
MPG Book Group in the UK

FOREWORD

I was thrilled to be asked to write a foreword for Chris's and Kevin's exciting new football quiz book. With over 1,000 questions, The Greatest Football Quiz Book certainly finds out how much you know about what has been happening in the game during the past 20 years. It certainly tested my own recollection of events.

I have many fond memories from my time as a player and now that I have hung up my football boots, I still enjoy following the game and keeping up with all the latest scores and signings. This book is excellent way to check up on all those important facts and figures from recent football history and with questions on every club in the country, there really is something for everyone.

I am honoured to note that Chris and Kevin have included a section about me which includes questions about my time with Spurs and as an England player as well as my recently published autobiography. The book also contains details on many other great players such as Jurgen Klinsmann, Alan Shearer, Wayne Rooney and my old England teammate, David

Beckham,

Chris and Kevin have once again put together an informative and entertaining reference guide. So, whether you are just starting out on your football journey or are a lifelong supporter of the beautiful game, all football fans should own a copy of this book.

Best wishes

Darren Anderton

Former Tottenham Hotspur & England Player

INTRODUCTION

I would first of all like to thank Darren Anderton for writing the foreword to this book; I have always been a big Anderton fan so I am very grateful for his help on this project. I would also like to thank everyone involved in the production of this book.

Football has always been a huge part of my life, from watching matches as a young boy, to going to Spurs matches with my dad and now writing many books on the sport.

You will see a list at the back of this book, listing all the books I have compiled, and the most common question has always been 'have you written one on football generally' – I hadn't, so here it is!

The book covers sections on teams, competitions, managers, players and much more. Kevin and I have tried our best to provide the reader with a mixture of easy, medium and hard questions, so this book is aimed at everyone, regardless of age. We always hope that there are facts and figures in our books that the readers didn't know, so you learn a little bit about your club.

I hope you enjoy testing your football knowledge; hopefully it should bring back some wonderful memories!

Best wishes

Chris Cowlin

THE FIRST PREMIER LEAGUE SEASON - 1992/1993

1.   Which French forward signed for Manchester United from Leeds in November 1992?

2.   Who was manager of Liverpool during this season?

3.   Which company were Tottenham's shirt sponsors during this season?

4.   Can you name the striker who finished this season as the League's top goalscorer with 22 Premier League goals?

5.   True or false: 22 teams were in the Premier League during this season?

6.   Which centre back signed for Arsenal from Everton in February 1993?

7.   Which East Anglian based team did Blackburn Rovers beat 7-1 at home during October 1992, recording the League's highest win of this season?

8.   Which was the highest London based club to finish in the Premier League during this season, finishing in fifth place?

9.   Can you name the Chelsea manager who was sacked in February 1993, after a string of poor results?

10.   How many League games did the champions Manchester United win during this season - 24, 25 or 26?

SIR ALEX FERGUSON

11. In which year did Sir Alex arrive at Old Trafford as Manchester United manager?

12. True or false: Sir Alex has managed Scotland in his managerial career?

13. Which midfielder did Sir Alex sign for Manchester United from Nottingham Forest in 1993 for £3.75 million?

14. How many times did Sir Alex win the Premier League Manager of the Month award in the 1990s whilst Manchester United manager?

15. For which Scottish team did Sir Alex play between 1967 and 1969?

16. In which year did Sir Alex lead Manchester United to the treble, winning the Premier League title, FA Cup and Champions League - 1997, 1998 or 1999?

17. Who was Sir Alex's assistant manager at Old Trafford during the 2002/2003 season, and then again from 2004-2008?

18. What is Sir Alex's middle name – Christopher, Chapman or Charles?

19. True or false: In 2008, Sir Alex became the third British manager to win the European Cup on more than one occasion?

20. In which year did Sir Alex win the BBC Sports Personality of the Year Coach Award?

FA CUP WINNERS – 1

Match up the year with the team that won the competition

21.	2001	Liverpool (beat West Ham 3-1 on penalties after a 3-3 draw)
22.	2002	Arsenal (beat Manchester 5-4 on penalties after a 0-0 draw)
23.	2003	Liverpool (beat Arsenal 2-1)
24.	2004	Chelsea (beat Everton 2-1)
25.	2005	Chelsea (beat Manchester United 1-0)
26.	2006	Arsenal (beat Chelsea 2-0)
27.	2007	Chelsea (beat Portsmouth 1-0)
28.	2008	Portsmouth (beat Cardiff City 1-0)
29.	2009	Arsenal (beat Southampton 1-0)
30.	2010	Manchester United (beat Millwall 3-0)

DARREN ANDERTON

31. How many Premier League seasons was Darren a Tottenham player?

32. True or false: Five different managers gave Darren's last five England caps to him?

33. How many League appearances did Darren make for Spurs in his career - 299, 319 or 339?

34. Against which team did Darren score his last Spurs League goal during November 2003 in a 2-1 away defeat?

35. How many international goals did Darren score for England in his career in his 30 international appearances – six, seven or eight?

36. What is the name of Darren's autobiography, released in 2010?

37. Which winners' medal did Darren collect at Wembley in 1999 whilst a Spurs player?

38. For which Midlands based club did Darren sign when he left White Hart Lane in 2004?

39. At which club did Darren finish his playing career?

40. Against which Yorkshire based club did Darren score Tottenham's only goal in the club's 1-0 home win during a Premier League match in March 1997?

LEAGUE CUP WINNERS – 1

Match up the year with the team that won the competition

41. 2001   Manchester United (beat Tottenham 4-1 on penalties after a 0-0 draw)

42. 2002   Tottenham (beat Chelsea 2-1)

43. 2003   Manchester United (beat Aston Villa 2-1)

44. 2004   Manchester United (beat Wigan Athletic 4-0)

45. 2005   Chelsea (beat Arsenal 2-1)

46. 2006   Blackburn Rovers (beat Tottenham 2-1)

47. 2007   Middlesbrough (beat Bolton Wanderers 2-1)

48. 2008   Liverpool (beat Manchester United 2-0)

49. 2009   Chelsea (beat Liverpool 3-2)

50. 2010   Liverpool (beat Birmingham City 5-4 on penalties after a 1-1 draw)

ALAN SHEARER

51.   How many full international England caps did Alan win for his country, scoring 30 goals between 1992 and 2000 – 60, 63 or 66?

52.   True or false: Alan has a Premier League champions' medal?

53.   In which year was Alan awarded the OBE?

54.   Against which club did Alan score a League hat-trick whilst playing for Blackburn Rovers, in a 5-1 home win during September 1995?

55.   At which club did Alan start his professional football career?

56.   How many goals did Alan score for England during Euro 96, finishing as the competition's Golden Boot Winner?

57.   In which year did Alan manage Newcastle United for a short spell?

58.   True or false: Alan scored 25 League goals in 31 matches during his first season at St. James Park, playing for Newcastle United during 1996/1997?

59.   Against which club did Newcastle United play in Alan's testimonial match in 2006?

60.   Alan is the Premier League's highest goalscorer with how many goals – 250, 260 or 270?

PREMIER LEAGUE SEASON – 2009/2010

61. Which club won the Premier League during this season?

62. Which team beat Wigan Athletic 9-1 at home during November 2009, recording the League's highest win of the season?

63. How many League goals did Carlos Tévez score in his first season at Manchester City – 21, 22 or 23?

64. Which manager was awarded the Manager of the Month award during January and March 2010?

65. Can you name the five London clubs that played in the Premier League during this season?

66. How many Premier League goals were scored during this season - 953, 1,053 or 1,153?

67. Which team did Stephen Carr captain during this season?

68. How many clean sheets did Manchester United keep during this season – 18, 19 or 20?

69. Which striker scored the fastest League goal of the season, after just 36 seconds, scoring for Sunderland against Tottenham during April 2010?

70. Can you name the three teams that were relegated at the end of the season?

ARSENAL

71. In which year did Nicklas Bendtner sign for The Gunners from FC Copenhagen?

72. What is the name of Arsenal's stadium?

73. Which Arsenal striker finished the 2002/2003 season as the club's highest League goalscorer with 24 goals?

74. Which team did The Gunners beat 6-0 at home in the Premier League during August 2010 with Theo Walcott scoring a hat-trick in the game?

75. Can you name the three players that scored double figures in the League during the 1997/1998 season?

76. Who took over at Highbury as club manager in June 1995?

77. How many times have Arsenal won the League Cup in their history?

78. In which year were Arsenal runners-up in the Champions League, losing 2-1 to Barcelona?

79. In which position did Arsenal finish in the Premier League during the 1992/1993 season, the first Premier League season – 8th, 10th or 12th?

80. Can you name the two goalkeepers that played in Arsenal's 38 League games during the 1999/2000 season?

ERIC CANTONA

81.   In which year was Eric born in Marseille – 1964, 1966 or 1968?

82.   How many FA Cup winners' medals did Eric pick up during his football career?

83.   For which country did Eric win 45 full international caps, scoring 20 goals?

84.   How many Premier League winners' medals did Eric pick up during his time at Manchester United?

85.   How many League goals did Eric score for Manchester United during the 1993/1994 season, his best tally during his time at the club?

86.   Which team were Manchester United playing when Eric was sent-off for kicking opponent Richard Shaw and then launching a 'kung-fu' style kick into the crowd, later being suspended from the game for four months?

87.   How many seasons did Eric play at Old Trafford, playing for Manchester United?

88.   From which club did Manchester United purchase Eric in 1992?

89.   What occupation did Eric take up after retiring from professional football?

90.   In which month during 1996 did Eric win the Premier League Player of the Month award?

TRANSFER FEES PAID

Match up the player with the fee and which club he joined

91. Tore Andre Flo   Blackburn Rovers to Newcastle United - £15 million (1996)

92. Cristiano Ronaldo   Blackburn Rovers to Tottenham Hotspur - £4 million (1999)

93. Alan Shearer   West Ham United to Chelsea - £11 million (2001)

94. Rio Ferdinand   Chelsea to Rangers - £12 million (2000)

95. Robbie Keane   Aston Villa to Manchester City - £12 million (2009)

96. Gareth Barry   Arsenal to Manchester City – £25 million (2009)

97. Andriy Shevchenko   Leeds United to Manchester United - £29.1 million (2002)

98. Tim Sherwood   Tottenham Hotspur to Liverpool - £19 million (2008)

99. Frank Lampard   AC Milan to Chelsea - £30 million (2006)

100. Emmanuel Adebayor   Manchester United to Real Madrid - £80 million (2009)

HARRY REDKNAPP

101. In which year did Harry guide Portsmouth to win the FA Cup, beating Cardiff City 1-0 at Wembley?

102. Which team did Harry manage from December 2004 until December 2005?

103. In which year was Harry born in London – 1945, 1946 or 1947?

104. What is Harry's real Christian name?

105. Which London team did Harry support when he was a young lad?

106. True or false: Harry is uncle to England midfielder Frank Lampard?

107. Can you name the two teams that Harry has both played for and managed in his football career?

108. What was the only honour Harry won whilst West Ham manager in 1999?

109. In which year was Harry appointed as Spurs boss?

110. In which position did Harry play during his playing days – defender, midfielder or striker?

MANCHESTER UNITED

111. In which year did Manchester United win the FIFA Club World Cup?

112. How many times did the club win the Premier League during the 1990s?

113. Which Bulgarian striker signed for United from Tottenham Hotspur in 2008?

114. How much was a match-day programme at Old Trafford during the 1985/1986 season?

115. Which company became the club's first ever shirt sponsors in the early 1980s?

116. In which year did Manchester United first win the League Cup?

117. Who was United's most successful captain in the club's history, captaining them from 1997 until 2005?

118. Who was manager of United before Alex Ferguson arrived at Old Trafford in 1986?

119. Can you name the three seasons in the 1990s that Manchester United did the double, winning the Premier League and FA Cup?

120. Who purchased the club in 2005?

KEVIN KEEGAN

121. At which club did Kevin start his professional playing career?

122. How many of the 18 England matches where Kevin was in charge of the national side did England win?

123. For which club did Kevin play between 1971 and 1977?

124. How many times did Kevin win the Premier League Manager of the Month award whilst managing Newcastle United during the 1994/1995 season?

125. Which League did Kevin win whilst managing Manchester City during the 2001/2002 season?

126. For which sports television company was Kevin appointed as their lead pundit during August 2009?

127. Which club did Kevin guide as manager to the Second Division title during the 1998/1999 season?

128. How many times did Kevin pick up an FA Cup winners' medal during his playing career?

129. What was the name of Kevin's song written by Chris Norman and Pete Spencer, which was released during June 1979 and peaked at number 31 in the UK charts

130. Which team did Kevin manage for a second time between January and September 2008?

ARSENE WENGER

131. In which year was Arsene born in Strasbourg, France?

132. How much did Arsene pay Paris Saint-Germain for Nicolas Anelka in February 1997?

133. How many times has Arsene led Arsenal to FA Cup success?

134. Which French team did Arsene manage between 1987 and 1995?

135. In which year was Arsene awarded the OBE for services to British football?

136. True or false: Arsene became the first non-British manager to win the Double in England (Premier League and FA Cup), having done so in 1998 and then again in 2002?

137. In which position did Arsene play during his playing days?

138. In which month during 2006 was Arsene appointed Gunners manager?

139. In which year did Arsene guide Arsenal to the Champions League final, losing 2-1 to Spanish side Barcelona?

140. How many times has Arsene won the Premier League Manager of the Year award?

PREMIER LEAGUE GOALSCORERS

Match the player with the number of goals he scored

141.	Teddy Sheringham	111
142.	Andy Cole	149
143.	Ian Wright	189
144.	Jimmy Hasselbaink	260
145.	Robbie Fowler	127
146.	Dion Dublin	174
147.	Dwight Yorke	163
148.	Alan Shearer	113
149.	Les Ferdinand	123
150.	Thierry Henry	147

ALEX McLEISH

151. What is Alex's nickname?

152. In which position did Alex play during his playing days?

153. True or false: When Alex was appointed manager of Birmingham City in 2007 it was his first experience in English football, not having played or managed in England before in his professional career?

154. In which month during 2009 was Alex awarded the Premier League Manager of the Month award whilst managing Birmingham City?

155. Who was Alex managing before he arrived at St. Andrews in 2007?

156. Which London club did Birmingham City beat 3-2 away in Alex's first game in charge of The Blues during December 2007?

157. To which position did Alex guide Birmingham City in the Premier League during the 2009/2010 season, the club's highest position in the League for over 50 years?

158. Which Scottish club did Alex manage from February 1998 until December 2001?

159. In which year was Alex born in Barrhead – 1957, 1958 or 1959?

160. To which position in the League did Alex guide Birmingham City in The Championship during the 2008/2009 season?

CHARLTON ATHLETIC

161. Can you name the manager who took charge at The Valley in January 2011?

162. Who was the club's Player of the Year in 2006?

163. Which company was the club's shirt sponsor between 2000 and 2002?

164. In which year was the club formed – 1900, 1905 or 1910?

165. True or false: Charlton have won the FA Cup in their history?

166. In which position did Charlton finish in the Premier League during the 2005/2006 season?

167. Which midfielder signed for Charlton from Ipswich during June 2003 for £750,000?

168. Which striker finished as the club's highest League scorer with 10 goals during the 2003/2004 season?

169. Which Charlton midfielder scored a brace for the club in a 4-2 home League win against West Ham during January 2003?

170. How much was a Charlton match-day programme at The Valley during the 2006/2007 season?

PLAYERS' NICKNAMES

Match up the player with his nickname

171.	Darren Anderton	Spiderman
172.	Matthew Le Tissier	Trigger
173.	David Beckham	Rock
174.	Carlos Tevez	Psycho
175.	Faustino Asprilla	The 'Guv' nor
176.	Marcel Desailly	Goldenballs
177.	Carlo Cudicini	Shaggy
178.	Jason McAteer	Tino
179.	Stuart Pearce	The Apache
180.	Paul Ince	Le God

MANCHESTER CITY

181. In which year did the club win the European Cup Winners' Cup?

182. Which goalkeeper wore the number 1 squad number during the 2010/2011 season?

183. Who managed City between 2001 and 2005?

184. What was the name of Manchester City's former ground?

185. Who is City's most capped player with 48 England caps?

186. True or false: City were League Cup finalists three times during the 1970s?

187. Which club did City beat 3-1 away from home on Boxing Day 2010?

188. Who was appointed City manager in 2009?

189. Which striker finished as the club's highest League scorer with 14 goals in 38 starts during the 2002/2003 season?

190. How many times have Manchester City won the FA Cup in their history?

DEFENDERS

Match the player with the club where he started his professional playing career

191.	Danny Shittu	Gillingham
192.	Julian Dicks	St Patrick's Athletic
193.	Paul McGrath	Everton
194.	Tony Gale	Shrewsbury Town
195.	Micky Adams	Bury
196.	Nigel Pearson	Fulham
197.	Micky Droy	Charlton Athletic
198.	Dave Watson	Birmingham City
199.	David Unsworth	Norwich City
200.	Alec Lindsay	Chelsea

TOTTENHAM HOTSPUR

201. Which club legend was appointed club manager in 2001?

202. In which year was the club formed – 1880, 1882 or 1884?

203. What does the club's Latin motto 'Audere est Facere' mean?

204. What did Spurs achieve in the 1960/1961 season, becoming the first team in the 20th century to do this?

205. With which team did Spurs draw 0-0 away in August 1992, the club's first ever Premier League match?

206. Which company became the club's first ever shirt sponsor in 1983?

207. How many times have Spurs won the FA Cup in their history?

208. Who was the first Spanish manager of Tottenham Hotspur, appointed in 2007?

209. Which German striker won the club's Player of the Year award at the end of the 1994/195 season?

210. Apart from Spurs, what is Tottenham's other nick name?

PREMIER LEAGUE CHAMPIONS – 1

Match up the season with the team that won the Premier League

211.	1992/1993	**Manchester United**
212.	1994/1996	**Chelsea**
213.	1996/1997	**Manchester United**
214.	1998/1999	**Manchester United**
215.	2000/2001	**Manchester United**
216.	2002/2003	**Manchester United**
217.	2004/2005	**Manchester United**
218.	2006/2007	**Manchester United**
219.	2008/2009	**Manchester United**
220.	2010/2011	**Blackburn Rovers**

CHELSEA

221. Which Russian purchased the club in 2003, helping the club to many successes?

222. Which Chelsea player won the club's Player of the Year award in 2007?

223. How many times did Chelsea win the Premier League whilst managed by Jose Mourinho?

224. In which year in the 1970s did Chelsea first win the FA Cup in their history?

225. Which company was the club's shirt sponsor from 1997 until 2001?

226. From which club did Chelsea sign Nicolas Anelka in 2008?

227. How much was a match-day programme at Stamford Bridge during the 1993/1994 season?

228. Who was Chelsea's manager between 1996 and 1998?

229. What are Chelsea's two nicknames?

230. What was Chelsea's average home gate during the 2009/2010 season, being the fifth highest in the Premier League during this season – 39,423, 40,423 or 41,423?

WAYNE ROONEY

231. What is Wayne's middle name – Chris, John or Mark?

232. How many seasons was Wayne an Everton player, before joining Manchester United?

233. True or false: Wayne scored 26 Premier League goals in 32 games during the 2009/2010 season at Manchester United?

234. In which year did Wayne win the BBC Young Sports Personality of the Year award?

235. Which squad number did Wayne wear for Manchester United during the 2010/2011 season?

236. What was the first trophy Wayne won whilst a Manchester United player?

237. What squad number was Wayne given when he arrived at Old Trafford?

238. Against which Midlands based club did Wayne score a Premier League brace in Manchester United's 3-1 home win during February 2011?

239. Against which team did Wayne make his Manchester United debut in a Champions League game in 2004, with The Red Devils winning 6-2 at home and Wayne scoring a hat-trick?

240. True or false: Wayne became the youngest player to play for England when he won his first cap against Australia during February 2003 when he was 17 years old, the same age at which he also became the youngest player to score a full England international goal?

SUNDERLAND

241. Who is Sunderland's all time top scorer in all competitions with 228 goals?

242. Which club did Sunderland beat 1-0 in the 1973 FA Cup final with Ian Porterfield scoring in the 30th minute?

243. In which year did Sunderland move from Roker Park to The Stadium of Light?

244. Which player holds the record for most League appearances of 527?

245. Which year was Sunderland formed – 1877, 1878 or 1879?

246. Which team did Sunderland beat 3-1 in the 1937 FA Cup final?

247. Which player made 36 appearances for the Republic of Ireland?

248. What is Sunderland's nickname?

249. Who were the club's sponsors from 1999 to 2007?

250. Which season did Sunderland first play in the Premier League?

PREMIER LEAGUE APPEARANCES

Match the player with the number of appearances he made

251.	Gareth Southgate	319
252.	Dennis Bergkamp	419
253.	Alan Shearer	315
254.	Gary Speed	379
255.	Andy Cole	535
256.	Ray Parlour	426
257.	Darren Anderton	372
258.	Trevor Sinclair	441
259.	Teddy Sheringham	414
260.	Nigel Martyn	361

BOLTON WANDERERS

261. In which year did Bolton move to the Reebok Stadium?

262. Who managed Bolton between 1999 and 2007?

263. True or false: Bolton were semi-finalists in the 2000 FA Cup?

264. In which position did Bolton finish in the Premier League at the end of the 2007/2008 season – 12th, 14th or 16th?

265. True or false: Bolton were the Premier Reserve League North Champions in 2007?

266. Who managed Bolton Wanderers between 1985 and 1992?

267. From which French club did Bolton sign Jay-Jay Okocha in 2002?

268. Which striker wore the number 14 shirt for Bolton during the 2010/2011 season?

269. Who were the club's shirt sponsors during the 1981/1982 season?

270. In which year during the 1990s was Bolton League Cup runners-up, losing 2-1 to Liverpool at Wembley Stadium?

THE GERMANS

Match the player with the club where he played

271.	Michael Ballack	Barnsley
272.	Karl-Heinz Riedle	Arsenal
273.	Fredi Bobic	Liverpool
274.	Thomas Helmer	Manchester City
275.	Savio Nsereko	Chelsea
276.	Jurgen Klinsmann	Sunderland
277.	Uwe Rosler	West Ham United
278.	Lars Leese	Derby County
279.	Stefan Schnoor	Bolton Wanderers
280.	Jens Lehmann	Tottenham Hotspur

STOKE CITY

281. Which year was Stoke City formed – 1863, 1864 or 1865?

282. Which team did Stoke City beat 2-1 to win the 1972 League Cup final?

283. True or false: Stoke City are considered to be the second oldest professional football club in the world?

284. How many League goals did Freddie Steele score for Stoke City?

285. In 1961 which famous player did Tony Waddington bring back to play for Stoke City after he had left 14 years earlier?

286. Which year did Stoke City move from the Victoria ground to the Britannia Stadium?

287. Which manager took Stoke City to the FA Cup final against Manchester City in May 2011?

288. What is the nickname of Stoke City?

289. Which local club is considered to be Stoke City's main rival?

290. Which two players made 606 appearances in all competitions for Stoke City?

GOALSCORING DEBUTS

Match the player with the club he made his goal scoring debut against

291. Frank Worthington for
      Bolton Wanderers,
      October 1977   **Chester City**

292. Robbie Keane for
      West Ham United,
      February 2011   **Leeds United**

293. Jermaine Defoe for
      Tottenham Hotspur,
      February 2004   **Bradford City**

294. Theo Walcott for
      Southampton, October 2005   **Chelsea**

295. John Toshack for
      Cardiff City, November 1965   **Leeds United**

296. Jim Cannon for
      Crystal Palace, March 1973   **Stoke City**

297. Francis Jeffers for
      Ipswich Town, March 2007   **Portsmouth**

298. Keith Curle for
      Bristol Rovers, August 1981   **Hull City**

299. Freddy Eastwood for
      Wolves, August 2007   **Leyton Orient**

300. Dennis Law for
      Manchester City, March 1961   **Blackpool**

ENGLAND

301. Which year did England win the World Cup?

302. Against which country did England suffer their heaviest defeat of 7-1 on 23 May 1954?

303. Which player made 125 appearances for England between 1970 and 1990?

304. Who was manager of England between 1963 and 1974?

305. Between 1958 and 1970 Bobby Charlton made 106 appearances for England how many goals did he score?

306. What is England's nickname?

307. With which other country is England the joint oldest national football team?

308. Who was the first England player to score two goals in a game at the 1954 World Cup finals?

309. Where do England play their home games?

310. Which player scored a hat-trick in the 4-2 win against West Germany in the World Cup final?

HONOURS

Match the club with the honour they won

311.	FA Cup 1927	Queens Park Rangers
312.	League Cup 1996	Ipswich Town
313.	FA Cup 2005	Cardiff City
314.	FA Cup 1958	Derby County
315.	Division One Champions 1960	Arsenal
316.	UEFA Cup 1981	Oxford United
317.	Division One Champions 1992	Aston Villa
318.	League Cup 1986	Burnley
319.	League Cup 1967	Leeds United
320.	Division One Champions 1975	Bolton Wanderers

LIVERPOOL

321.   Who was Liverpool's manager from 1959 to 1974?

322.   What was the transfer fee when Andy Carroll signed from Newcastle United on 31 January 2011?

323.   What is the title of the club's famous anthem?

324.   How many League and cup games did Ian Callaghan play for Liverpool – 757, 857 or 957?

325.   What is the name of Liverpool's ground?

326.   Which player holds the record for the fastest Premier League hat-trick in 4 minutes 32 seconds against Arsenal in the 1994/95 season?

327.   In 2005 which Italian team did Liverpool beat on penalties after a 3-3 draw in the Champions League final?

328.   What is Liverpool's nickname?

329.   Who are the main rivals of Liverpool?

330.   Which Liverpool striker made his international debut for Wales in May 1980?

NEWCASTLE UNITED

331. Who is Newcastle United's all time top scorer with 206 goals in all competitions between 1996 and 2006?

332. Which honour did Newcastle United win in May 2010?

333. Which striker was signed from Luton Town in 1971?

334. What is the name of Newcastle United's ground?

335. In August 2005 how much did Newcastle United pay for Michael Owen from Real Madrid?

336. How many goals did Jackie Milburn score in 396 competitive matches for Newcastle United?

337. Who was manager of Newcastle United from 1999 to 2004?

338. Which two players won the Premier League Golden Boot whilst playing for Newcastle United?

339. What are the supporters of Newcastle United called?

340. Who are Newcastle United's main rivals on Tyneside?

BLACKPOOL

341.   Which year was Blackpool Football Club founded –
        1883, 1885 or 1887?

342.   Which year did Blackpool first play in the Premier
        League?

343.   Which club did Blackpool beat 4-3 to win the 1953 FA
        Cup final?

344.   Who became manager of Blackpool in May 2009?

345.   What is the name of Blackpool's ground?

346.   In 2009 how much was the transfer fee paid for Charlie
        Adam from Rangers?

347.   Who is Blackpool's most capped player with 43 for
        England?

348.   How many League goals did Jimmy Hampson score in
        his Blackpool career?

349.   How many League appearances did Jimmy Armfield
        make for Blackpool between 1954 and 1971?

350.   Which player played for Blackpool from 1997 to 2001
        and returned again in 2009?

MIDDLESBROUGH

351. Which player has made a record 602 appearances in all competitions for Middlesbrough?

352. Which year did Middlesbrough move from Ayresome Park to the Riverside Stadium?

353. Which club did Middlesbrough beat 2-1 to win the League Cup final at the Millennium Stadium in 2004?

354. Which manager took Middlesbrough to the 2006 UEFA cup final in Eindhoven where they lost 4-0 to Sevilla?

355. How many goals in all competitions did George Camsell score in his Middlesbrough career – 325, 335 or 345?

356. Which year was Middlesbrough founded – 1874, 1876 or 1878?

357. True or false: Middlesbrough were the only team to beat Manchester United at Old Trafford in the 1998-99 treble winning season?

358. During the 2007/08 season, which manager paid £12 million for the Brazilian Afonso Alves?

359. Which club beat Middlesbrough 2-0 in the 1997 FA Cup final?

360. Can you name the three Middlesbrough players who played in the 2006 FIFA World Cup?

GROUNDS - 1

Match up the team with where they play their home games

361.	Fulham	The Valley
362.	Sunderland	Riverside Stadium
363.	Sheffield United	Hillsborough
364.	Leicester City	Molineux
365.	Nottingham Forest	Bramall Lane
366.	Middlesbrough	Craven Cottage
367.	Blackpool	City Ground
368.	Wolves	Stadium of Light
369.	Charlton Athletic	Bloomfield Road
370.	Sheffield Wednesday	Walkers Stadium

BLACKBURN ROVERS

371. Which season was Blackburn Rovers first crowned Premier League Champions?

372. Which Blackburn player made 56 FA Cup appearances between 1949 and 1969?

373. Which year was Blackburn Rovers founded – 1875, 1877 or 1879?

374. How many League goals did Simon Garner score in his Blackburn Rovers career?

375. How many Premier League appearances did Alan Shearer make for Rovers scoring 112 goals?

376. Which club do Blackburn Rovers play against and this match is known as the East Lancashire Derby?

377. Before Blackburn played at Ewood Park in 1890 where did they play their home games?

378. Who was manager of Blackburn from 1960 to 1967?

379. Can you name three of the years Blackburn won the FA Cup?

380. Which player made 593 (3) League appearances for Rovers between 1970 and 1987?

EVERTON

381. Which player made 751 appearances for Everton between 1981 and 1997?

382. How many spells did Howard Kendall have as Everton manager?

383. Which European honour did Everton win in 1985?

384. Which year was Everton founded as St Domingo's FC before being renamed a year later?

385. Which player was signed by David Moyes for £15 million in September 2008?

386. Which company became Everton's shirt sponsor in 2004?

387. Which club is Everton's main rival?

388. Which player scored 383 goals in all competitions for Everton from 1924 to 1937?

389. Who was Everton's longest serving player, playing from 1929 to 1953?

390. How many League goals did Dixie Dean score in the season of 1927/28 a record that still stands today?

TEAM NICKNAMES – 1

Match up the team with their nickname

391.	Norwich City	The Clarets
392.	Sheffield Wednesday	The Whites
393.	Hull City	The Red Devils
394.	Swindon Town	The Owls
395.	Watford	The Rams
396.	Stoke City	The Tigers
397.	Burnley	The Canaries
398.	Derby County	The Robins
399.	Leeds United	The Hornets
400.	Manchester United	The Potters

WEST BROMWICH ALBION

401. True or false: The club's stadium is the highest of all the football League grounds at an altitude of 551 feet above sea level?

402. Can you name three of the five years in which the club has won the FA Cup?

403. What was unveiled at The Hawthorns on 11 July 2003 in Jeff Astle's memory?

404. Who became West Brom's record signing during August 2008, costing £4.7 million from Real Mallorca?

405. Who holds the record for appearing 574 times in League matches from 1963 to 1981?

406. What is the club's official nickname?

407. To which team did West Brom lose 1-0 in the Championship promotion play-off final at Wembley Stadium during May 2007?

408. Can you name the legendary Baggies' striker who holds the record for scoring the most number of League goals for the club?

409. Fred Morris was the first West Brom player to do what in season 1919/20?

410. Which 'Lee' scored the The Baggies' first ever goal in the Premier League?

LONDON DERBIES

411. Which two clubs contest the North London Derby?

412. The first ever League match between Arsenal and Tottenham Hotspur was in the First Division on 4 December 1909 what was the score?

413. What did Terry Dyson (August 1916), Ted Drake (October 1934) and Alan Sunderland (December 1978) all achieve in a North London Derby?

414. Which player has played in the most North London Derbies?

415. What did Jimmy Robertson achieve in the North London Derby?

416. Which four teams contest the West London Derbies?

417. In the Premier League in March 2006 who scored Fulham's goal in a 1-0 over Chelsea?

418. Which two players both scored a brace in the 4-4 draw between Charlton Athletic and Millwall in December 2009?

419. True or false: When West Ham United beat Millwall 3-1 AET this was the first ever meeting between the clubs in the League Cup?

420. Which two clubs contest the East London Derby?

ASTON VILLA

421. Which player scored the only and winning goal for Villa against Bayern Munich to win the 1982 European Cup?

422. Who was manager of Villa when they won the European Cup in 1982?

423. True or false: Villa manager Jozef Venglos was the first manager not from Britain or Ireland to take charge of a top-flight club in England?

424. Which club are Villa's rivals in the Second City derby?

425. In which position did Villa finish in the Premier League in 2010?

426. Which year was Villa founded – 1870, 1872 or 1874?

427. Which honour did Villa win in 1981?

428. True or false: Since the formation of the premier League in 1992 to 2011 Villa have only been relegated once?

429. What is the club's motto?

430. What did Archie Hunter achieve for Villa in 1887?

PAUL GASCOIGNE

431. For which Italian club did Paul play between 1992 and 1995?

432. What is Paul's middle name?

433. How many goals did Paul score in his 57 full international caps for England - 10, 12 or 14?

434. Which team did Paul manage for a very brief spell in 2005?

435. In which year did Paul win the BBC Sports Personality of the Year award?

436. How many Premier League goals did Paul score for Everton during his playing spell between 2000 and 2002?

437. Can you name the only honour Paul won whilst a Tottenham player?

438. In which year was Paul born in Gateshead – 1965, 1966 or 1967?

439. For which Scottish team did Paul play between 1995 and 1998?

440. Which BBC television quiz show, along with other sporting heroes, was Paul a contestant on during July 2009?

WEST HAM UNITED

441. Which defender wore the number 15 shirt during the 2010/2011 season?

442. Who was the club's captain during the 1992/1993 season?

443. Who were the club's kit sponsors between 1993 and 1997?

444. In which position in the Premier League did West Ham finish during the 1998/1999 season, the club's highest finish in Premier League history?

445. In which year did the club last win the FA Cup?

446. Can you name the two most used nicknames for West Ham United?

447. Who was the club's first ever non-English manager, appointed in 1989?

448. In which year did Jermain Defoe leave Upton Park and join Tottenham?

449. Who managed West Ham United between 2001 and 2003?

450. Which Hammers striker won the Hammer of the Year award in 2005?

WIGAN ATHLETIC

451. Which year did Wigan Athletic move from Springfield Road to the DW Stadium?

452. Wigan's first ever Premier League match was in August 2005 a home game they lost 1-0, who were the opponents?

453. Which club does Wigan Athletic rent the DW Stadium to?

454. Who was Wigan Athletic's first ever manger staying with the club five years until 1937?

455. Which honour did Wigan win in 1997?

456. Which team defeated Wigan 9-1 on 22 November 2009 to record their heaviest League defeat?

457. Which Wigan player scored 70 League goals from 1998 to 2003?

458. Which player did Wigan sell to Manchester United in June 2009 for £16 million?

459. Which year did Wigan Athletic become a Football League club?

460. How many consecutive League appearances did Jimmy Bullard make for Wigan from January 2003 to November 2005?

FULHAM

461. Which team did Fulham lose to 2-0 in the 1975 FA Cup final?

462. Who were Fulham's shirt sponsors from 2007 to 2010?

463. Who had the longest spell as Fulham manager, which lasted 15 years from 1909 to 1924?

464. When Craven Cottage was under renovation 2002 to 2004 where did Fulham play their home matches?

465. Which Spanish club did Fulham lose to 2-1 in the 2010 Europa League Cup final with Simon Davies scoring?

466. Which year was Fulham founded – 1879, 1881 or 1883?

467. Which honour did Fulham win in 2003?

468. True or false: Fulham are the oldest professional football club in London?

469. Which year did Mohamed Al-Fayed purchase Fulham FC?

470. Which Fulham player was called up by Fabio Capello to play for England in 2010?

LES FERDINAND

471. How many England goals did Les score in his 17 caps for his country?

472. In which position did Les play during his playing days?

473. What was Les's nickname during his playing days?

474. How many League goals did Les score for Newcastle United in his first season at St. James' Park during the 1995/1996 season – 23, 24 or 25?

475. For which club did Les play during the 2003/2004 season?

476. True or false: Les picked up an FA Cup winners' medal during his playing career?

477. For which London club did Les play between 1987 and 1995?

478. In which year was Les born in London - 1965, 1966 or 1967?

479. How much did Tottenham pay for Les in 1997, a club Les supported as a young boy?

480. True or false: Les scored the 10,000th Premier League goal?

STRIKERS

*Match the striker with the club where they finished
their professional playing career*

481. John Radford   Barnet

482. Bobby Charlton   Chelsea

483. Cyrille Regis   Preston North End

484. Frank Stapleton   Newcastle United

485. Peter Osgood   Chester City

486. Alan Taylor   Blackburn Rovers

487. Kevin Keegan   Maritimo

488. Rodney Marsh   Brighton & Hove Albion

489. Martin Chivers   Norwich City

490. John Richards   Tampa Bay Rowdies

BIRMINGHAM CITY

491. Which position did Birmingham finish in the Premier League in 2009/10?

492. Which team did Birmingham beat 2-1 to win the 2011 League Cup final at Wembley?

493. Which player between 1908 and 1928 made 491 League appearances for Birmingham City?

494. Between 1920 and 1935 how many goals did Joe Bradford score for the Blues – 239, 249 or 259?

495. What was the transfer fee when Birmingham signed Emile Heskey from Liverpool in 2004?

496. Who were Birmingham's shirt sponsors from 1995 to 2001?

497. In 1970 which player did Birmingham sell to Everton for then a British record of £350,000?

498. Which year was Birmingham City founded?

499. In 1978 Trevor Francis became the first £1 million transfer in the Country, which club bought him?

500. Which team did Birmingham beat on penalties in the 2001/02 play-off final to gain promotion to the Premier League?

THE FRENCH

Match the player with the club he played for

501.	Fabian Barthez	Birmingham City
502.	Zoumana Camara	Arsenal
503.	Bruno Cheyrou	Manchester United
504.	Mattieu Flamini	Fulham
505.	Christian Karembeu	Sunderland
506.	Frank Leboeuf	Leeds United
507.	Christophe Dugarry	Liverpool
508.	Eric Roy	Bolton Wanderers
509.	Bruno N'Gotty	Chelsea
510.	Steve Marlet	Middlesbrough

RYAN GIGGS

511.   How many full international goals did Ryan score in his 64 appearances for Wales - 12, 14 or 16?

512.   What was Ryan's surname before he changed it to Giggs when he was 16 years-old?

513.   In which season during the 1990s did Ryan score 13 Premier League goals, his highest tally in a League season whilst he has played for Manchester United?

514.   Where in the UK was Ryan born in 1973?

515.   True or false: In January 2011, Ryan was named Manchester United's greatest ever player by a world wide poll conducted by Manchester United's official magazine?

516.   What squad number did Ryan wear for Manchester United during the 2010/2011 season – 7, 11 or 17?

517.   Against which team did Ryan score his 100th Manchester United League goal in a 4-1 win during December 2007?

518.   True or false: Ryan has never been sent off for Manchester United in his career?

519.   How many Champions League winners' medals has Ryan won whilst he has been at Old Trafford?

520.   True or false: Ryan has made more appearances for Manchester United than any other player in the club's history?

SCOTLAND

521. Which two players have both scored 30 goals for Scotland?

522. Which German managed Scotland from 2002 to 2004?

523. Who is the longest serving manager of Scotland being in charge for 70 matches?

524. Can you name Scotland's other three group opponents in the 1990 FIFA World Cup finals?

525. What is the name of Scotland's supporters?

526. Which Country beat Scotland 7-0 in the 1954 FIFA World Cup finals?

527. Who is the only player to make over 100 appearances for Scotland?

528. Who is Scotland's most capped goalkeeper making 91 appearances?

529. What is the name of Scotland's national football stadium?

530. What do the years 1984 and 2004 have in common for Scotland's football team?

IPSWICH TOWN

531.   Where does Ipswich Town play their home games?

532.   Which manager was appointed in January 2011?

533.   In which year did Town win the UEFA Cup - 1981, 1982 or 1983?

534.   In which two colours do Ipswich Town play?

535.   Which defender was the club's Player of the Year during the 2005/2006 season?

536.   In which position in the Premier League did Town finish in the 1992/1993 season, the first ever Premier League season?

537.   How much was a match-day programme at Ipswich Town Football Club during the 2010/2011 season?

538.   Which London team did Ipswich beat 1-0 in the 1978 FA Cup final?

539.   Which former player managed Town from 1994 until 2002?

540.   In which year did Town last appear in the Premier League?

NORWICH CITY

541. Which year were floodlights installed at Carrow Road at a cost of £9,000?

542. Who was Norwich's Player of the Year in 2005 and again in 2007?

543. Who is Norwich's longest serving manager from November 1980 to November 1987?

544. Which honour did The Canaries win in 1962 and again in 1985?

545. Which player wore the number 9 shirt in the 2010/11 season?

546. Norwich City's record victory was a 10-2 win in the Division Three (South) in 1930, who were their opponents?

547. How many appearances in all competition did Ron Ashman make for Norwich between 1947 and 1964?

548. Who were the club's sponsors from 2006 to 2008?

549. Which team is Norwich's main rival and make up the other half of the East Anglian Derby?

550. True or false: Paul Lambert was the manager of Colchester United who inflicted a 7-1 home defeat on Norwich the first day of the 2009/10 season, he then went on to manage City to the 2009/10 League One title?

WHERE DO WE PLAY - 1?

Can you name the clubs that play at the following grounds?

551. Moss Rose

552. Oakwell

553. London Road

554. Valley Parade

555. Brunton Park

556. The County Ground

557. Kassam Stadium

558. Priestfield Stadium

559. Spotland

560. B2net Stadium

LEEDS UNITED

561. Who took over as Leeds Chairman in 2005?

562. How many League and Cup goals did Peter Lorimar score in his Leeds career?

563. In which year was Leeds United founded?

564. True or false: Between 1965 and 1974 Leeds never finished outside of the top four in Division One?

565. Who is Leeds longest serving manager from 1 March 1961 to 4 July 1974?

566. How many players did Leeds United use in the season of 2006/07?

567. Which player scored 168 League goals in his Leeds career?

568. What is the name of Leeds United's stadium?

569. Who was Leeds United's manager for the 2010/11 season?

570. In which competition were Leeds United runners-up in 1965, 1970 and 1973?

WOLVES

571.   What did Wolves achieve in 1988?

572.   How many appearances in all competitions did Derek Parkin make for Wolves between 1968 and 1982?

573.   Which Wolves player made 105 appearances for England, 91 as captain between 1939 and 1959?

574.   How much did Wolves pay for Kevin Doyle from Reading in June 2009 and Steven Fletcher from Burnley in June 2010?

575.   Between 1967 and 1975 which player made 18 European appearances for Wolves?

576.   Which year did Mick McCarthy become manager of Wolves?

577.   Who is Wolves top goalscorer in all competitions with 306 between 1986 and 1999?

578.   Which cup did Wolves win in 1974 and again in 1980?

579.   Which club beat Wolves to win the 1972 UEFA Cup final 3-2 on aggregate?

580.   Which year was Wolves founded – 1875, 1877 or 1978?

GLENN HODDLE

581. Which team did Glenn manage between 2004 and 2006?

582. For which team was Glenn a player/manager in 1994 when he was a FA Cup finalist, losing 4-0 in the final to Manchester United?

583. Which team is the only one that Glenn hasn't managed who he played for in his career?

584. In which year was Glenn born in Hayes - 1955, 1956 or 1957?

585. Which team beat Glenn Hoddle's Tottenham 2-1 in the 2002 League Cup final?

586. How many full international goals did Glenn score for England during his 53 caps – 8, 11 or 14?

587. Which tournament did Glenn win whilst England manager in 1997?

588. How many League goals did Glenn score in his 64 League games for Swindon between 1991 and 1993?

589. In which position did Glenn mostly play during his playing career?

590. In which year was Glenn appointed England manager?

CLUB NICKNAMES

Can you name the club from their nickname?

591. **The Millers**

592. **The Bulls**

593. **The Cherries**

594. **The Glovers**

595. **The Imps**

596. **The Pilgrims**

597. **The Pirates**

598. **The Railwaymen**

599. **The Saddlers**

600. **The Shakers**

RAFAEL VAN DER VAART

601. Which squad number did Rafael wear for Tottenham during the 2010/2011 season?

602. How much did Rafael cost Spurs when he arrived at White Hart Lane in August 2010?

603. From which Spanish giants did Tottenham sign Rafael?

604. What nationality is Rafael?

605. True or false: Rafael scored a brace for Tottenham against Aston Villa at home and away in the two League meetings during the 2010/2011 season, with Tottenham winning 2-1 in each match?

606. Against which club did Rafael score his first Tottenham goal, in a 3-1 home League win during September 2010?

607. Which Spurs manager signed Rafael for the club?

608. At which Dutch club did Rafael start his professional football career, playing there from 2000 until 2005?

609. What is Rafael's middle name – Ferdinand, Sherwood or Campbell?

610. Against which club did Rafael score Tottenham's goal in the 64th minute in the 1-1 League draw during November 2010?

SOUTHAMPTON

611. Which club did Southampton beat 1-0 to win the 1976 FA Cup final with Bobby Stokes scoring?

612. Who was Southampton's manager when they won the 1976 FA Cup?

613. Which player scored 185 League goals for Southampton in his two spells with the club?

614. Which Southampton player was the first midfielder to score 100 goals in the Premier League?

615. How many appearances in all competitions did Terry Paine make for The Saints between 1956 and 1974?

616. While a Southampton player how many caps for England did Peter Shilton win?

617. Before Southampton moved to St Mary's Stadium in 2001 where did they play their home matches?

618. Who was appointed manager of Southampton in September 2010?

619. Which year was Southampton founded – 1881, 1883 or 1885?

620. In 1901 against which club did Albert Brown score seven goals for Southampton in one match?

BOBBY ROBSON

621. In which position did Bobby play during his playing days?

622. Which Dutch team did Bobby go on to manage after his eight year spell as England boss in 1990?

623. Which England manager did Bobby take over from in 1982?

624. True or false: Bobby was the guest of honour at the FA Cup Final at Wembley Stadium when Portsmouth beat Cardiff City 1-0 during Amy 2008?

625. How many times did Bobby guide Porto to the Portuguese Championship during his time as manager at the club?

626. At which club did Bobby have two playing spells during his football career, first in the 1950s and then again in the 1960s?

627. How many full England goals did Bobby score in his 20 appearances for his country between 1957 and 1962 – three, four or five?

628. Which team did Bobby guide to win the 1981 UEFA Cup?

629. What was Bobby's middle name – William, Christopher or Kevin?

630. Which was the only team Bobby managed in the Premier League?

PREMIER LEAGUE CHAMPIONS – 2

Match up the season with the team that won the
Premier League during that season

631. 1993/1994   Manchester United

632. 1995/1996   Arsenal

633. 1997/1998   Manchester United

634. 1999/2000   Chelsea

635. 2001/2002   Chelsea

636. 2003/2004   Manchester United

637. 2005/2006   Manchester United

638. 2007/2008   Arsenal

639. 2009/2010   Arsenal

640. 2011/2012   Manchester United

DERBY COUNTY

641.   Who were Derby's shirt sponsors between 1995 and 1998?

642.   What is the club's nickname?

643.   In which year did the club move to Pride Park?

644.   Which goalkeeper won the Derby County Player of the Year in 2000?

645.   Which year was the last time that Derby was crowned champions of the top flight in England?

646.   Which former Leicester City and Wales midfielder was Derby's captain during the 2010/2011 season?

647.   Which midfielder won the Derby County Player of the Year award in 2003?

648.   In which year was Derby County formed – 1882, 1884 or 1886?

649.   Who managed Derby between 2003 and 2005?

650.   What is the name of Derby's mascot?

THIERRY HENRY

651. In which year did Thierry leave Arsenal to join Spanish giants Barcelona?

652. From which Italian club did Thierry join Arsenal in 1999?

653. How many times was Thierry a FA Cup winner whilst an Arsenal player?

654. Against which team did Thierry score an Arsenal League hat-trick in the club's 4-2 home win during May 2006?

655. In which year was Thierry born – 1976, 1977 or 1978?

656. Against which team did Thierry score an Arsenal League hat-trick in the club's 7-0 home win during January 2006?

657. How many Premier League goals did Thierry score for The Gunners in the 2003/2004 season, in his 37 starts – 28, 29 or 30?

658. For which French club did Thierry play between 1994 and 1999?

659. What is Thierry's middle name – Daniel, David or Damien?

660. How many League goals did Thierry score for Arsenal in his career, in his 254 appearances for The Gunners – 172, 173 or 174?

BARNSLEY

661. In which year did Barnsley first play Premier League football and reach the top tier of English football for the first time in their history?

662. Who managed Barnsley between 1994 and 1998?

663. What is the club's official nickname?

664. In which year was the club formed – 1887, 1889 or 1891?

665. Can you name Barnsley's youngest player to appear for the club, aged 15 years and 45 days, making his appearance against Ipswich Town during September 2008?

666. Who is the club's most capped player, winning 25 caps whilst at the club between 1990 and 1995?

667. Where does Barnsley play their home matches?

668. True or false: Barnsley has only ever spent one season in the Premier League in their history?

669. Which striker did Barnsley sell to Blackburn Rovers during December 1998 for £4.5 million?

670. In which year was Mark Robins appointed club manager?

GIANFRANCO ZOLA

671. In which year did Gianfranco join Chelsea?

672. Which London team did Gianfranco manage between 2008 and 2010?

673. How many League goals did Gianfranco score for Chelsea in his last season at Stamford Bridge, during the 2002/2003 season, which was his highest League tally during his time with the club?

674. Which Italian club did Gianfranco join when he left Stamford Bridge in 2003?

675. How many FA Cup winners' medals did Gianfranco win whilst a Chelsea player?

676. In which year was Gianfranco awarded the OBE for services to football?

677. True or false: Gianfranco played Premier League football for West Ham United in his career?

678. Which Chelsea manager signed Gianfranco in November 1996?

679. What squad number did Gianfranco wear during his first season at Chelsea, during the 1996/1997 season?

680. From which Italian team did Chelsea sign Gianfranco in 1996?

MERSEYSIDE DERBIES

681. At the start of the 1984/85 season Everton played Liverpool in the FA Charity Shield at Wembley with Everton winning 1-0 due to an own goal by which Liverpool player?

682. What was the score when Liverpool played Everton at Anfield in the 1935/36 season?

683. What is the record attendance in a Merseyside Derby, which took place at Goodison Park on 18 September 1948 in a Division One match?

684. Who is the only player to win the FA Cup with both Liverpool and Everton?

685. Which player is the top goalscorer in the Merseyside Derby with 25 goals?

686. William Cuff manager of Everton in the early 1900s had how many wins over Liverpool – 10, 13 or 16?

687. Which Everton player is top goalscorer with 18 goals in the Merseyside Derby?

688. Which Everton player made 41 appearances in the Merseyside Derby between 1981 and 1998?

689. Which two goalkeepers have kept 15 clean sheets each in the Merseyside Derby?

690. Which team won the FA Charity Shield in 1986 Liverpool or Everton?

CAPS FOR MY COUNTRY - 1

Match up the player with how many caps and goals
he won/scored for his country

691. Matt Holland   79 Dutch Caps, 37 goals

692. Richard Wright   66 England Caps, 5 goals

693. David Ginola   129 Danish Caps, 1 goal

694. Dennis Bergkamp   7 England Caps, 0 goals

695. Gianfranco Zola   63 England Caps, 30 goals

696. Teddy Sheringham   49 Republic of Ireland Caps, 5 goals

697. Tony Adams   2 England Caps, 0 goals

698. Tony Cottee   17 French Caps, 3 goals

699. Alan Shearer   35 Italian Caps, 10 goals

700. Peter Schmeichel   51 England Caps, 11 goals

SHEFFIELD WEDNESDAY

701. Which club does Sheffield Wednesday play in the Steel City Derby?

702. Which honour did The Owls win in 1991?

703. Which Wednesday player won the Football Writers' Association Footballer of the Year in 1993?

704. How many goals did Sheffield Wednesday score in the 1958/59 season – 86, 96 or 106?

705. Who was manager of Sheffield Wednesday from October 1977 to May 1983?

706. True or false: Kevin Pressman was sent off after just 33 seconds in August 2000?

707. Which year was Sheffield Wednesday founded – 1865, 1867 or 1869?

708. How many caps did Nigel Worthington win for Northern Ireland while being a Wednesday player?

709. The Owls record home win in the League is 9-1 in Division One on 13 December 1930, who were their opponents?

710. In the 1993 FA Cup semi-final what was the score when Sheffield Wednesday beat Sheffield United?

TONY ADAMS

711. Which club did Tony manage between November 2003 and November 2004?

712. How many Premier League winners' medals did Tony pick up during his time at Arsenal?

713. Which team did Tony manage between October 2008 and February 2009?

714. True or false: Tony only ever played professional football for Arsenal in his career?

715. How old was Tony when he was made Arsenal captain?

716. How many full international England goals did Tony score for England during his career - five, six or seven?

717. What is Tony's middle name – Alexander, John or Philip?

718. Against which Scottish team did Arsenal and Tony play in his testimonial during May 2002?

719. In which year did Tony form his own charity, the Sporting Chance Clinic, a charitable foundation aimed at providing treatment, counselling and support for sportsmen and women suffering from drink, drug or gambling addictions?

720. How many times did Tony lift the FA Cup for Arsenal as club captain?

QUEENS PARK RANGERS

721.   In what year was Queens Park Rangers founded?

722.   Which manager took charge of Queens Park Rangers in March 2010 and took them to the Premier League in 2011?

723.   Which team were Queens Park Rangers first League opponents on 9 September 1899, a game they lost 1-0?

724.   In 1979 which teenager did Queens Park Rangers sell to Arsenal for £1 million?

725.   What is the name of Queens Park Rangers' stadium?

726.   Which player scored 44 goals for QPR in the 1966/67 season?

727.   Who is QPR's most capped player, with 52 appearances for Northern Ireland?

728.   Which club paid £6 million for Les Ferdinand in June 1995?

729.   How many goals in all competitions did George Goddard score for QPR between 1926 and 1934?

730.   Which player made 519 League appearances for QPR between 1950 and 1963?

NOTTINGHAM FOREST

731. Which Forest manager guided them to the 1979 and 1980 European Cup wins?

732. Which player made 692 appearances for Forest in all competitions?

733. Forest's first ever League match was on 3 September 1892 against Everton away what was the score – 1-1, 2-2 or 3-3?

734. What was the transfer fee when Forest bought Pierre van Hooijdonk from Celtic in March 1997?

735. Who started sponsoring Forest shirts in 2009?

736. Which Forest player made 76 appearances for England while at the club?

737. Who was manager of Forest from 1997 to 1999?

738. How many goals in all competitions did Grenville Morris score in his Forest career – 217, 227 or 237?

739. Which honour did Forest win in 1898 and again in 1959?

740. Who are Forest's main rivals whose ground Meadow Lane is just across the River Trent?

COVENTRY CITY

741. Which year was Coventry City founded – 1883, 1885 or 1887?

742. Which year did Coventry move to The Ricoh Arena after 106 years at Highfield Road?

743. Who was Coventry's Player of the Season in 1971/72 – Ernie Hunt, Willie Carr or Tommy Hutchinson?

744. How many League goals did Clarrie Bourton score for Coventry from 1931 to 1937?

745. Who was manger of Coventry from 1996 to 2001?

746. In 1970, under Noel Cantwell, in what position did Coventry City finish in the First Division?

747. Who is Coventry's most capped player with 109 for Trinidad & Tabago?

748. Which Coventry goalkeeper made 507 League appearances from 1984 to 2000?

749. In 1987 which club did Coventry beat in the FA Cup final 3-2 to win the FA Cup for the very first time in their history?

750. What is Coventry City's nickname?

THE DUTCH

Match the player with the club he played for

751.	Ed de Goey	Aston Villa
752.	Wim Jonk	Manchester United
753.	Clyde Wijnhard	Sheffield Wednesday
754.	Bryan Roy	Arsenal
755.	Jordi Cruyff	Newcastle United
756.	Arnold Muhren	Leeds United
757.	Paul Bosvelt	Ipswich Town
758.	Denis Bergkamp	Nottingham Forest
759.	Wilfred Bouma	Manchester City
760.	Patrick Kluivert	Chelsea

STEVE BRUCE

761. With which club did Steve start his professional playing career in 1979?

762. What was the transfer fee when Manchester United signed Steve from Norwich City in December 1987?

763. How many appearances did Steve make for Manchester United in all competitions – 404(4), 414(4) or 424(4)?

764. What is Steve's middle name – Roger, Rodney or Robin?

765. Which club was Steve manger of between 2001 and 2007?

766. How many times did Steve win the Premier League title with Manchester United?

767. Steve was born on 31 December in which year – 1960, 1962 or 1964?

768. With which Yorkshire club did Steve finish his professional playing career in 1999?

769. Against which club did Steve make his Manchester United debut on 19 December 1987 winning 2-1?

770. True or false: Steve only ever made one full international appearance for England?

WHERE DO WE PLAY – 2?

Can you name the clubs that play at the following grounds?

771.   Meadow Lane

772.   The Globe Arena

773.   Vale Park

774.   Prenton Park

775.   Griffin Park

776.   The Keepmoat Stadium

777.   Roots Hall

778.   Boundary Park

779.   Adams Park

780.   Brisbane Road

WALES

781. How many caps did Gary Speed win for Wales scoring seven goals?

782. Which player has made a record 92 appearances for Wales between 1982 and 1998?

783. Who was manager of Wales between 2004 and 2010?

784. True or false: Wales reached the Quarter-Finals of the FIFA 1958 World Cup?

785. How many goals did Ian Rush score in his 73 appearances for Wales 18, 28 or 38?

786. Which player scored Wales' goal in the 4-1 defeat away to Switzerland on 12 October 2010?

787. Where do Wales play their home games?

788. What is Wales' nickname?

789. In 1933 Wales played their first game outside of the United Kingdom, the game ended 1-1, which country did they play?

790. Which player scored on his debut for Wales in 1984 when they defeated England 1-0?

LEICESTER CITY

791. Who became manager of Leicester City in 2010?

792. Between 1920 and 1935 which player made 528 League appearances for Leicester City?

793. Which player scored after nine seconds against Preston North End in April 2006?

794. Which Leicester manager took them to the Premier League in 1994?

795. Which honour did Leicester win in 1997 and 2000 under the management of Martin O'Neill?

796. Which year did Leicester City move to The Walker Stadium after spending 111 years at Filbert Street?

797. What is Leicester City's nickname?

798. Can you name the former Leicester City player who hosts Match of the Day?

799. Who were Leicester City's shirt sponsors from 1987 to 2001?

800. How many goals did Arthur Chandler score in all competitions for Leicester City – 273, 283 or 293?

GOALKEEPERS

Match the player with the club he started his professional playing career with

801.	Pat Jennings	Manchester City
802.	Peter Shilton	West Ham United
803.	Gordon Banks	Wolverhampton Wanderers
804.	Neville Southall	Leicester City
805.	Ray Clemence	Peterborough United
806.	Joe Corrigan	Bury
807.	Peter Bonetti	Watford
808.	David Seaman	Chelsea
809.	Mervyn Day	Chesterfield
810.	Phil Parkes	Scunthorpe United

DENNIS BERGKAMP

811.   In which year did Dennis arrive at Highbury?

812.   At which Dutch club did Dennis start his football career?

813.   How many times did Dennis win the charity shield whilst an Arsenal player?

814.   How many Premier League goals did Dennis score for Arsenal during the 1997/1998 season, his highest League tally during a season during his Arsenal career?

815.   True or false: In 2007 Dennis was inducted into the English Football Hall of Fame, the first ever Dutch player to receive the honour?

816.   Which Gunners manager signed Dennis for Arsenal?

817.   What does Dennis have a fear of – flying, flies or bees?

818.   For which Italian club did Dennis play during 1993 and 1995?

819.   True or false: Dennis won five FA Cup winners medals whilst at Arsenal?

820.   In which year did Dennis win the PFA Players' Player of the Year award?

PLAYERS HONOURS

Match up the player with some of the honours he won during his career

821.	Gary Mabbutt	**FA Cup winner in 2008 (Portsmouth)**
822.	Diego Forlan	**League Cup winner in 2000 (Leicester City)**
823.	Colin Hendry	**FA Cup winner in 1990, 1994 and 1996 (Manchester United)**
824.	Dennis Wise	**League Cup winner in 1999 (Tottenham Hotspur)**
825.	Savo Milosevic	**League Cup winner in 1995 and 2001 (Liverpool)**
826.	Robbie Fowler	**Premier League winner in 2003 (Manchester United)**
827.	Sol Campbell	**FA Cup winner in 1991 (Tottenham Hotspur)**
828.	David James	**Premier League winner in 2005 (Blackburn Rovers)**
829.	Robbie Savage	**League Cup winner in 1996 (Aston Villa)**
830.	Steve Bruce	**FA Cup winners in 1997 and 2000 (Chelsea)**

WATFORD

831. Which player has made a record 415 League appearances for Watford?

832. How many League goals did Luther Blissett score in his Watford career – 128, 138 or 148?

833. What position did Watford finish in the First Division in 1983?

834. Which Watford manager 1977-87 and 1997-2001 went on to become Chairman of the club?

835. Which famous pop star is a life long fan of Watford?

836. Which club is considered to be Watford's rival?

837. Which goalkeeper made 291 appearances for The Hornets?

838. Which manager took Watford to the Premier League in 2006?

839. Which year was Watford founded – 1880, 1881 or 1882?

840. Where do Watford play their home matches?

DAVID O'LEARY

841. In which position did David play during his playing days?

842. True or false: David once played for Leeds United?

843. Which Midlands club did David manage between 2003 and 2006?

844. What is David's middle name – Anthony, Anton or Andrew?

845. In which year was David appointed Leeds United manager?

846. How many appearances did David make for Arsenal from 1975 to 1993?

847. Where in London was David born in 1958?

848. David played at international level for the Republic of Ireland, how many appearances did he make – 58, 68 or 78?

849. Which two honours did David win while at Arsenal in 1993?

850. True or false: David's brother Pierce also played professional football?

GROUNDS – 2

Match up the team with where they play their home games

851.	Blackburn Rovers	Goodison Park
852.	Stoke City	Fratton Park
853.	Queens Park Rangers	Boundary Park
854.	Manchester City	Pride Park Stadium
855.	West Bromwich Albion	Ewood Park
856.	Derby County	Loftus Road
857.	Everton	Selhurst Park
858.	Crystal Palace	The Hawthorns
859.	Portsmouth	City Of Manchester Stadium
860.	Oldham Athletic	Britannia Stadium

HULL CITY

861. Can you name the stadium that Hull moved to in 2002?

862. What is the club's nickname?

863. In what year in their history did the club first play top flight football?

864. Which player holds the record for most League appearances with 520?

865. What is the name of the club's mascot?

866. In what year was Hull City formed?

867. Which team did Hull City beat 1-0 with Dean Windass scoring in the Championship Play-off final at Wembley in May 2008?

868. Which team did Hull City beat 2-1 on 16 August 2008 the opening day of the Premier League season?

869. At which ground did Hull City play between 1945 and 2002?

870. Which two colours do the club wear during their home matches?

TEDDY SHERINGHAM

871. At which Essex based club did Teddy finish his football career, at the end of the 2007/2008 season?

872. How many Premier League winners' medals did Teddy win whilst a Manchester United player?

873. How many full international goals did Teddy score for England in his 51 games for his country?

874. At which London club did Teddy start his football career?

875. What is Teddy's middle name?

876. What was Teddy the oldest player in Premier League history to do, whilst playing for Portsmouth during the 2003/2004 season?

877. How many Premier League goals did Teddy score for Manchester United in his career – 21, 31 or 41?

878. In which year was Teddy awarded the MBE?

879. At which club did Teddy have two playing spells, the first between 1992 and 1997 and the second between 2001 and 2003?

880. In which position did Teddy play during his playing days?

PORTSMOUTH

881. Which club did Portsmouth beat 1-0 with Nwankwo Kanu scoring to win the 2008 FA Cup?

882. What is the club's nickname?

883. Which south coast club are Portsmouth's main rivals?

884. Which two years were Portsmouth the First Division Champions?

885. How many League goals did Guy Whittingham score for Portsmouth in the 1992/93 season?

886. Which player between 1946 and 1965 made 834 appearances in all competitions for Portsmouth?

887. How many League goals did Peter Harris score for Portsmouth between 1946 and 1960 – 174, 184 or 194?

888. In July 2008, which player did Portsmouth sign from Liverpool for £11 million?

889. Where does Portsmouth play their home matches?

890. Who was manager of Portsmouth 2002-04 and 2005-08?

ROBERTO MANCINI

891. Which Italian club did Roberto manage between 2004 and 2008?

892. For which Premier League team did Roberto play only four League matches during early 2001?

893. In which year was Roberto appointed Manchester City manager?

894. Which manager did Roberto take over from when he was appointed Manchester City boss?

895. In which month during 2010 was Roberto awarded the Manager of the Month award?

896. In which position in the Premier League did Roberto guide Manchester City in his first season in charge at the club?

897. True or false: Roberto guided Manchester City to their highest ever Premier League finish in their history in his first season in charge at the club?

898. Which club did Roberto face as his opponents, when he took charge of Manchester City for the first time, winning the game 2-0 at home?

899. What nationality is Roberto?

900. In which year was Roberto awarded the Player of the Year award in his country?

NORTHERN IRELAND

901. Which goalkeeper made 119 appearances for Northern Ireland?

902. Where does Northern Ireland play their home matches?

903. How many goals did Iain Dowie score in his 59 appearances for Northern Ireland?

904. Who was manager of Northern Ireland 1967-71 and 1980-94?

905. What is Northern Ireland's nickname?

906. True or false: Northern Ireland won the last Home Championship held in 1984?

907. Which player scored the goal in Northern Ireland's 1-0 win over the hosts Spain in the 1982 FIFA World Cup finals?

908. Which player scored 13 goals for Northern Ireland in trying to qualify for Euro 2008?

909. What was the score when Northern Ireland beat England in the 2006 World Cup qualifier at Windsor Park – 1-0, 2-0 or 2-1?

910. Who took over as manager of Northern Ireland in 2007?

CLUB NICKNAMES – 2

Can you name the club from their nicknames?

911.   The Chairboys

912.   The Cobblers

913.   The Grecians

914.   The O's

915.   The Seagulls

916.   The Shrews

917.   The Terriers

918.   The Valiants

919.   The Shrimps

920.   The Gulls

RUUD GULLIT

921. What nationality is Ruud?

922. What was the only honour Ruud won whilst Chelsea manager?

923. True or false: Ruud became the first non-British manager to win a major trophy in England?

924. How many League goals did Ruud score for Chelsea in his football career – two, four or six?

925. True or false: Ruud was awarded the Chelsea Player of the Year award at the end of his first season at Stamford Bridge, at the end of the 1995/1996 season?

926. Which Premier League team did Ruud manage during the 1998/1999 season?

927. True or false: Ruud has been married three times?

928. For which Italian team did Rudd play between 1987 and 1993 and then again in the 1994/1995 season?

929. Which Chelsea manager signed Ruud for the club in July 1995?

930. Which Dutch team did Ruud manager from August 2004 until May 2005?

CRYSTAL PALACE

931. Crystal Palace's nickname is The Eagles but what was their former nickname?

932. How many appearances in all competitions did Jim Cannon make for Crystal palace – 660, 670 or 680?

933. Which player scored a hat-trick in 6 minutes 48 seconds against Wolves in the FA Cup Fourth Round Replay at Selhurst Park in February 2010?

934. Who was crystal Palace's Player of the Year in 2004 and again in 2005?

935. Who was manager of Crystal Palace 1976-80 and 1998-99?

936. From 1930 to 1936 how many goals in all competitions did Peter Simpson score for Crystal Palace – 143, 153 or 163?

937. Which player was sold to Everton for £8.6 million in May 2006?

938. Which club beat Crystal Palace in the 1990 FA Cup final replay 1-0 after a 3-3 draw?

939. Which year was Crystal Palace founded – 1901, 1903 or 1905?

940. Who were Palace's first ever opponents at Selhurst Park in 1924 a game they lost 1-0?

MIDFIELDERS

*Match the player with the club where he finished his
professional playing career*

941.	Bryan Robson	Leyton Orient
942.	Liam Brady	Rangers
943.	Graeme Souness	Stourbridge
944.	Glenn Hoddle	Middlesbrough
945.	Johnny Haynes	Doncaster Rovers
946.	Ray Wilkins	West Ham United
947.	Colin Bell	Tottenham Hotspur
948.	Danny Blanchflower	Maritzburg
949.	Willie Carr	San Jose Earthquakes
950.	Billy Bremner	Chelsea

IAN WRIGHT

951. Which club did Ian make more League appearances for Arsenal or Crystal Palace?

952. How many appearances did Ian make for England scoring nine goals?

953. With which club did Ian finish his professional playing career in 2000?

954. How many League goals did Ian score while at Arsenal from 1991 to 1998?

955. Besides playing for Crystal Palace and Arsenal, for which other London club did Ian play?

956. What is Ian's middle name – Eric, Ernie or Edward?

957. What was the transfer fee when Ian signed for Arsenal on 24 September 1991?

958. Which England manager gave Ian his England debut in February 1991 a 2-0 home win against Cameroon?

959. Which honour was Ian awarded in 2002?

960. Which Football club does Ian support?

TEAM NICKNAMES – 2

Match up the team with their nickname

961.	Leicester City	The Cottagers
962.	West Bromwich Albion	The Blues
963.	Southampton	The Trotters
964.	Liverpool	The Foxes
965.	Reading	The Latics
966.	Coventry City	The Saints
967.	Fulham	The Baggies
968.	Wigan Athletic	The Reds
969.	Ipswich Town	The Sky Blues
970.	Bolton Wanderers	The Royals

DIDIER DROGBA

971. What squad number did Didier wear for Chelsea during the 2010/2011 season?

972. From which French club did Chelsea sign Didier in July 2004?

973. For which country does Didier play?

974. In which position does Didier play?

975. How much did Chelsea pay for Didier in July 2004?

976. Against which team did Didier score a Chelsea hat-trick in the club's 6-0 home League win during August 2010?

977. In which year was Didier born – 1977, 1978 or 1979?

978. Against which team did Didier score a Chelsea hat-trick in the club's 8-0 home League win during May 2010?

979. How many League goals did Didier score for Chelsea in his first season at Stamford Bridge, during the 2004/2005 season?

980. Didier scored 29 League goals for Chelsea in 32 appearances during the 2009/2010 season; can you name the Chelsea player that scored 22 goals in 36 starts in the same season for The Blues?

SHEFFIELD UNITED

981.   What is the club's nickname?

982.   True or false: Sheffield United were in the Premier
        League during the 2006/2007 season?

983.   How many times has Sheffield United won the FA Cup
        in their history?

984.   Who was in charge at Bramall Lane as club manager
        from 1999 until 2007?

985.   In which year during the 1980s did Sheffield United
        win Division Four?

986.   Which striker did Sheffield United pay a club record £4
        million for to Everton in August 2007?

987.   Which United player made a record 631 League
        appearances for the club between 1948 and 1966?

988.   Who managed Sheffield United between 1988
        and1995?

989.   Which company were the club's main shirt sponsors
        from 2004 until 2006?

990.   In which year was the club formed – 1897, 1898 or
        1899?

CAPS FOR MY COUNTRY – 2

Match up the player with how many caps and goals he won/scored for his country

991. David Seaman   116 French Caps, 3 goals

992. Anders Limpar   59 Italian Caps, 16 goals

993. Ally McCoist   59 England Caps, 0 goals

994. Efan Ekoku   73 England Caps, 1 goal

995. Marcel Desailly   75 England Caps, 0 goals

996. Paul Gascoigne   61 Scottish Caps,
                                  19 goals

997. Frank Leboeuf   58 Swedish Caps, goals

998. Sol Campbell   20 Nigerian Caps,
                                  6 goals

999. Gianluca Vialli   57 England Caps,
                                  10 goals

1000. Des Walker   50 French Caps, 5 goals

ANSWERS

THE FIRST PREMIER LEAGUE SEASON - 1992/1993

1. Eric Cantona
2. Graeme Souness
3. Holsten
4. Teddy Sheringham: One goal for Nottingham Forest and 21 for Tottenham Hotspur
5. True
6. Martin Keown
7. Norwich City
8. Queens Park Rangers
9. Ian Porterfield
10. 24 (from 42 games)

SIR ALEX FERGUSON

11. 1986
12. True: From September 1985 until June 1986
13. Roy Keane
14. Nine: August 1993, October 1994, February 1996, March 1996, February 1997, October 1997, January 1999, April 1999 and August 1999
15. Rangers
16. 1999
17. Carlos Queiroz
18. Chapman
19. True
20. 1999

FA CUP WINNERS – 1

21.	2001	Liverpool (beat Arsenal 2-1)
22.	2002	Arsenal (beat Chelsea 2-0)
23.	2003	Arsenal (beat Southampton 1-0)

24.	2004	Manchester United (beat Millwall 3-0)
25.	2005	Arsenal (beat Manchester 5-4 on penalties after a 0-0 draw)
26.	2006	Liverpool (beat West Ham 3-1 on penalties after a 3-3 draw)
27.	2007	Chelsea (beat Manchester United 1-0)
28.	2008	Portsmouth (beat Cardiff City 1-0)
29.	2009	Chelsea (beat Everton 2-1)
30.	2010	Chelsea (beat Portsmouth 1-0)

DARREN ANDERTON

31. 12

32. True: vs Czech Republic (18/11/98) by Glenn Hoddle, vs France (10/02/99) by Howard Wilkinson, vs France (02/09/00) by Kevin Keegan, vs Italy (15/11/00) by Peter Taylor and vs Sweden (10/11/01) by Sven-Göran Eriksson

33. 299: 273 (26)

34. Arsenal

35. Seven

36. Take Note

37. The League Cup (The Worthington Cup)

38. Birmingham City

39. Bournemouth (finishing his career in the 2008/2009 season)

40. Leeds United

LEAGUE CUP WINNERS – 1

41.	2001	Liverpool (beat Birmingham City 5-4 on penalties after a 1-1 draw)
42.	2002	Blackburn Rovers (beat Tottenham 2-1)
43.	2003	Liverpool (beat Manchester United 2-0)
44.	2004	Middlesbrough (beat Bolton Wanderers 2-1)

45.	2005	Chelsea (beat Liverpool 3-2)
46.	2006	Manchester United (beat Wigan Athletic 4-0)
47.	2007	Chelsea (beat Arsenal 2-1)
48.	2008	Tottenham (beat Chelsea 2-1)
49.	2009	Manchester United (beat Tottenham 4-1 on penalties after a 0-0 draw)
50.	2010	Manchester United (beat Aston Villa 2-1)

ALAN SHEARER

51. 63
52. True: With Blackburn Rovers in the 1994/1995 season
53. 2001
54. Coventry City
55. Southampton
56. Five
57. 2009 (April-May)
58. True
59. Celtic
60. 260

PREMIER LEAGUE SEASON – 2009/2010

61. Chelsea
62. Tottenham Hotspur (there was also an 8-0 win for Chelsea against Wigan Athletic)
63. 23
64. David Moyes (managing Everton)
65. Arsenal, Chelsea, Fulham, Tottenham Hotspur and West Ham United
66. 1,053
67. Birmingham City
68. 19

69. Darren Bent

70. Portsmouth, Burnley and Hull City

ARSENAL

71. 2005

72. Emirates Stadium

73. Thierry Henry

74. Blackpool

75. Dennis Bergkamp (16), Marc Overmars (12) and Ian Wright (10)

76. Bruce Rioch

77. Twice: 1987 and 1993

78. 2006

79. 10th

80. David Seaman (24 starts) and Alex Manninger (14 starts and 1 substitute appearance)

ERIC CANTONA

81. 1966

82. Two: 1994 and 1996

83. France

84. Four: 1992/1993, 1993/1994, 1995/1996 and 1996/1997

85. 18

86. Crystal Palace

87. Five: 1992/1993, 1993/1994, 1994/1995, 1995/1996 and 1996/1997

88. Leeds United

89. Acting

90. March

TRANSFER FEES PAID

91.	Tore Andre Flo	Chelsea to Rangers - £12 million (2000)
92.	Cristiano Ronaldo	Manchester United to Real Madrid - £80 million (2009)
93.	Alan Shearer	Blackburn Rovers to Newcastle United - £15 million (1996)
94.	Rio Ferdinand	Leeds United to Manchester United - £29.1 million (2002)
95.	Robbie Keane	Tottenham Hotspur to Liverpool - £19 million (2008)
96.	Gareth Barry	Aston Villa to Manchester City - £12 million (2009)
97.	Andriy Shevchenko	AC Milan to Chelsea - £30 million (2006)
98.	Tim Sherwood	Blackburn Rovers to Tottenham Hotspur - £4 million (1999)
99.	Frank Lampard	West Ham United to Chelsea - £11 million (2001)
100.	Emmanuel Adebayor	Arsenal to Manchester City - £25 million (2009)

HARRY REDKNAPP

101. 2008
102. Southampton
103. 1947
104. Henry
105. Arsenal
106. True
107. West Ham United and Bournemouth
108. Intertoto Cup winners

109. *2008*

110. *Midfielder*

MANCHESTER UNITED

111. *2008*

112. *Five: in 1993, 1994, 1996, 1997 and 1999*

113. *Dimitar Berbatov*

114. *40p*

115. *Sharp Electronics*

116. *1992*

117. *Roy Keane*

118. *Ron Atkinson*

119. *1993/1994, 1995/1996, and 1998/1999*

120. *Malcolm Glazer*

KEVIN KEEGAN

121. *Scunthorpe United*

122. *Seven*

123. *Liverpool*

124. *Two: August 1994 and February 1995*

125. *Division One*

126. *ESPN*

127. *Fulham*

128. *Once: in 1974 (with Liverpool)*

129. *Head Over Heels in Love*

130. *Newcastle United*

ARSENE WENGER

131. *1949*

132. *£500,000*

133. *Four: 1998, 2002, 2003 and 2005*

134. Monaco

135. 2003

136. True

137. Sweeper

138. September

139. 2006

140. Three: 1998, 2002 and 2004

PREMIER LEAGUE GOALSCORERS

141.	Teddy Sheringham	147
142.	Andy Cole	189
143.	Ian Wright	113
144.	Jimmy Hasselbaink	127
145.	Robbie Fowler	163
146.	Dion Dublin	111
147.	Dwight Yorke	123
148.	Alan Shearer	260
149.	Les Ferdinand	149
150.	Thierry Henry	174

ALEX McLEISH

151. Big Eck

152. Central defender

153. True

154. December

155. Scotland

156. Tottenham Hotspur

157. 9th

158. Hibernian

159. 1959

160. Second (runners-up to winners Wolves)

CHARLTON ATHLETIC

161. Chris Powell
162. Darren Bent
163. Redbus
164. 1905
165. True: in 1947
166. 13th
167. Matt Holland
168. Jason Euell
169. Scott Parker
170. £3

PLAYERS' NICKNAMES

171.	Darren Anderton	Shaggy
172.	Matthew Le Tissier	Le God
173.	David Beckham	Goldenballs
174.	Carlos Tevez	The Apache
175.	Faustino Asprilla	Tino
176.	Marcel Desailly	Rock
177.	Carlo Cudicini	Spiderman
178.	Jason McAteer	Trigger
179.	Stuart Pearce	Psycho
180.	Paul Ince	The 'Guv' nor

MANCHESTER CITY

181. 1970
182. Shay Given
183. Kevin Keegan
184. Maine Road
185. Colin Bell

186. *True: Winning the competition in 1970 and 1976 and being a finalist in 1974*

187. **Newcastle United**

188. **Roberto Mancini**

189. **Nicolas Anelka**

190. **Four: 1904, 1934, 1956 and 1969**

DEFENDERS

191.	Danny Shittu	**Charlton Athletic**
192.	Julian Dicks	**Birmingham City**
193.	Paul McGrath	**St Patrick's Athletic**
194.	Tony Gale	**Fulham**
195.	Micky Adams	**Gillingham**
196.	Nigel Pearson	**Shrewsbury Town**
197.	Micky Droy	**Chelsea**
198.	Dave Watson	**Norwich City**
199.	David Unsworth	**Everton**
200.	Alec Lindsay	**Bury**

TOTTENHAM HOTSPUR

201. **Glenn Hoddle**

202. **1882**

203. **To Dare is to Do**

204. **They were the first club in the 20th century to achieve the League and FA Cup Double**

205. **Southampton**

206. **Holsten**

207. **Eight: in 1901, 1921, 1961, 1962, 1967, 1981, 1982 and 1991**

208. **Juande Ramos**

209. **Jurgen Klinsmann**

210. **The Lilywhites**

PREMIER LEAGUE CHAMPIONS - 1

211.	1992/1993	Manchester United
212.	1994/1996	Blackburn Rovers
213.	1996/1997	Manchester United
214.	1998/1999	Manchester United
215.	2000/2001	Manchester United
216.	2002/2003	Manchester United
217.	2004/2005	Chelsea
218.	2006/2007	Manchester United
219.	2008/2009	Manchester United
220.	2010/2011	Manchester United

CHELSEA

221. Roman Abramovich
222. Michael Essien
223. Two: in 2004/2005 and 2005/2006
224. 1970
225. Autoglass
226. Bolton Wanderers
227. £1.50
228. Ruud Gullit
229. The Blues and The Pensioners
230. 41,423

WAYNE ROONEY

231. Mark
232. Two: (2002/2003 and 2003/2004)
233. True
234. 2002
235. 10
236. League Cup (2006)

237.   8

238.   Aston Villa

239.   Fenerbahce

240.   True

SUNDERLAND

241.   Bobby Gurney

242.   Leeds United

243.   1997

244.   Jim Montgomery

245.   1879

246.   Preston North End

247.   Charlie Hurley

248.   The Black Cats

249.   Reg Vardy Car Dealership Company

250.   1995/96

PREMIER LEAGUE APPEARANCES

251.   Gareth Southgate   426

252.   Dennis Bergkamp   315

253.   Alan Shearer   441

254.   Gary Speed   535

255.   Andy Cole   414

256.   Ray Parlour   379

257.   Darren Anderton   319

258.   Trevor Sinclair   361

259.   Teddy Sheringham   419

260.   Nigel Martyn   372

BOLTON WANDERERS

261.   1997

262. Sam Allardyce

263. True

264. 16th

265. True

266. Phil Neal

267. Paris Saint-Germain

268. Kevin Davies

269. Bolton Evening News

270. 1995

THE GERMANS

271.	Michael Ballack	Chelsea
272.	Karl-Heinz Riedle	Liverpool
273.	Fredi Bobic	Bolton Wanderers
274.	Thomas Helmer	Sunderland
275.	Savio Nsereko	West Ham United
276.	Jurgen Klinsmann	Tottenham Hotspur
277.	Uwe Rosler	Manchester City
278.	Lars Leese	Barnsley
279.	Stefan Schnoor	Derby County
280.	Jens Lehmann	Arsenal

STOKE CITY

281. 1863

282. Chelsea

283. True: Notts County being the oldest

284. 140

285. Stanley Matthews

286. 1997

287. Tony Pulis

288. The Potters

289. Port Vale

290. Eric Skeels and Frank Mountford

GOALSCORING DEBUTS

291. Frank Worthington for Bolton Wanderers,
      October 1977   **Stoke City**

292. Robbie Keane for West Ham United,
      February 2011   **Blackpool**

293. Jermaine Defoe for Tottenham Hotspur,
      February 2004   **Portsmouth**

294. Theo Walcott for Southampton,
      October 2005   **Leeds United**

295. John Toshack for Cardiff City,
      November 1965   **Leyton Orient**

296. Jim Cannon for Crystal palace,
      March 1973   **Chelsea**

297. Francis Jeffers for Ipswich Town,
      March 2007   **Hull City**

298. Keith Curle for Bristol Rovers,
      August 1981   **Chester City**

299. Freddy Eastwood for Wolves,
      August 2007   **Bradford City**

300. Dennis Law for Manchester City,
      March 1961   **Leeds United**

ENGLAND

301. 1966

302. Hungary

303. Peter Shilton

304. Sir Alf Ramsey

305. 49

306. Three Lions

307. Scotland

308. Ivor Broadis

309. Wembley Stadium

310. Geoff Hurst

HONOURS

311.	FA Cup 1927	Cardiff City
312.	League Cup 1996	Aston Villa
313.	FA Cup 2005	Arsenal
314.	FA Cup 1958	Bolton Wanderers
315.	Division One Champions 1960	Burnley
316.	UEFA Cup 1981	Ipswich Town
317.	Division One Champions 1992	Leeds United
318.	League Cup 1986	Oxford United
319.	League Cup 1967	Queens Park Rangers
320.	Division One Champions 1975	Derby County

LIVERPOOL

321. Bill Shankly

322. £35 million

323. 'You'll Never Walk Alone'

324. 857

325. Anfield

326. Robbie Fowler

327. AC Milan

328. The Reds

329. Everton

330. Ian Rush

NEWCASTLE UNITED

331.   Alan Shearer

332.   Football League Championship

333.   Malcolm McDonald

334.   St. James' Park

335.   £16 million

336.   200

337.   Bobby Robson

338.   Andy Cole in 1994 and Alan Shearer in 1997

339.   The Toon Army

340.   Sunderland

BLACKPOOL

341.   1887

342.   2010

343.   Bolton Wanderers

344.   Ian Holloway

345.   Bloomfield Road

346.   £500,000

347.   Jimmy Armfield

348.   248

349.   569

350.   Brett Ormerod

MIDDLESBROUGH

351.   Tim Williamson

352.   1995

353.   Bolton Wanderers

354.   Steve McClaren

355.   345

356.   1876

357. True

358. Gareth Southgate

359. Chelsea

360. Stewart Downing, Mark Schwarzer and Mark Viduka

GROUNDS - 1

361.	Fulham	Craven Cottage
362.	Sunderland	Stadium of Light
363.	Sheffield United	Bramall Lane
364.	Leicester City	Walkers Stadium
365.	Nottingham Forest	City Ground
366.	Middlesbrough	Riverside Stadium
367.	Blackpool	Bloomfield Road
368.	Wolves	Molineux
369.	Charlton Athletic	The Valley
370.	Sheffield Wednesday	Hillsborough

BLACKBURN ROVERS

371. 1994/95

372. Ronnie Clayton

373. 1875

374. 168 (1978 to 1992)

375. 138

376. Burnley

377. Leamington Road

378. Jack Marshall

379. 1884, 1885, 1886, 1890, 1891 and 1928

380. Derek Fazackerley

EVERTON

381. Neville Southall

382.   Three: 1981-87, 1990-93 and 1997-98

383.   European Cup Winners' Cup

384.   1878

385.   Marouane Fellaini

386.   Chang Beer

387.   Liverpool

388.   Dixie Dean

389.   Ted Sagar (Goalkeeper)

390.   60

TEAM NICKNAMES - 1

391.   Norwich City   The Canaries

392.   Sheffield Wednesday   The Owls

393.   Hull City   The Tigers

394.   Swindon Town   The Robins

395.   Watford   The Hornets

396.   Stoke City   The Potters

397.   Burnley   The Clarets

398.   Derby County   The Rams

399.   Leeds United   The Whites

400.   Manchester United   The Red Devils

WEST BROMWICH ALBION

401.   True

402.   1888, 1892, 1931, 1954 and 1968

403.   A large pair of gates named The Jeff Astle Gates

404.   Borja Valero

405.   Tony Brown

406.   The Baggies

407.   Derby County

408.   Tony Brown (218 League goals from 1963-81)

409. End the season as the leading goalscorer in the First Division

410. Lee Marshall

LONDON DERBIES

411. Arsenal and Tottenham Hotspur

412. Arsenal 1-0 Tottenham Hotspur

413. They all scored hat-tricks

414. David O'Leary

415. Only player to score for both Arsenal and Tottenham Hotspur

416. Brentford, Chelsea, Fulham and Queens Park Rangers

417. Luis Boa Morte

418. Steve Morison for Millwall and Deon Burton for Charlton Athletic

419. True

420. Millwall and West Ham United

ASTON VILLA

421. Peter Withe

422. Tony Barton

423. True

424. Birmingham City

425. Sixth

426. 1874

427. First Division Champions

428. False: They have never been relegated

429. 'Prepared'

430. First player to score in every round of the FA Cup

PAUL GASCOIGNE

431. Lazio

432. John

433. *10*

434. *Kettering Town*

435. *1990*

436. *One*

437. *FA Cup (1991)*

438. *1967*

439. *Rangers*

440. *The Weakest Link*

WEST HAM UNITED

441. *Matthew Upson*

442. *Julian Dicks*

443. *Dagenham Motors*

444. *Fifth*

445. *1980*

446. *The Hammers and The Irons*

447. *Lou Macari (he is Scottish)*

448. *2004*

449. *Glenn Roeder*

450. *Teddy Sheringham*

WIGAN ATHLETIC

451. *1999*

452. *Chelsea with Hernan Crespo scoring in the 94th minute*

453. *Wigan Warrior rugby league team*

454. *Charlie Spencer*

455. *Football League Third Division Championship*

456. *Tottenham Hotspur*

457. *Andy Liddell*

458. *Antonio Valencia*

459. *1978*

460.   123

FULHAM

461.   West Ham United

462.   LG

463.   Phil Kelso

464.   Loftus Road, Queens Park Rangers ground

465.   Atletico Madrid

466.   1879

467.   UEFA Intertoto Cup

468.   True

469.   1997

470.   Bobby Zamora

LES FERDINAND

471.   5

472.   Striker

473.   Sir Les

474.   25

475.   Leicester City

476.   False: Les was never an FA Cup winner with any of his clubs

477.   Queens Park Rangers

478.   1966

479.   £6 million

480.   True

STRIKERS

481.   John Radford   Blackburn Rovers

482.   Bobby Charlton   Preston North End

483.   Cyrille Regis   Chester City

484.   Frank Stapleton   Brighton & Hove Albion

485.	Peter Osgood	Chelsea
486.	Alan Taylor	Norwich City
487.	Kevin Keegan	Newcastle United
488.	Rodney Marsh	Tampa Bay Rowdies
489.	Martin Chivers	Barnet
490.	John Richards	Maritimo

BIRMINGHAM CITY

491.	Ninth
492.	Arsenal
493.	Frank Womack
494.	249
495.	£6.25 million
496.	Auto Windscreens
497.	Bob Latchford
498.	1875
499.	Nottingham Forest
500.	Norwich City

THE FRENCH

501.	Fabian Barthez	Manchester United
502.	Zoumana Camara	Leeds United
503.	Bruno Cheyrou	Liverpool
504.	Mattieu Flamini	Arsenal
505.	Christian Karembeu	Middlesbrough
506.	Frank Leboeuf	Chelsea
507.	Christophe Dugarry	Birmingham City
508.	Eric Roy	Sunderland
509.	Bruno N'Gotty	Bolton Wanderers
510.	Steve Marlet	Fulham

RYAN GIGGS

511. 12

512. Wilson

513. 1993/1994

514. Cardiff

515. True

516. 11

517. Derby County

518. True: However, he has been sent-off once playing international football for Wales

519. Two: in 1999 and 2008

520. True

SCOTLAND

521. Dennis Law (1958-1974) and Kenny Dalglish (1971-1986)

522. Berti Vogts

523. Craig Brown (1993-2002)

524. Cost Rica lost 1-0, Sweden won 2-1 and Brazil lost 1-0

525. The Tartan Army

526. Uruguay

527. Kenny Dalglish with 102 appearances

528. Jim Leighton

529. Hampden Park

530. They did not qualify for the FIFA World Cup finals

IPSWICH TOWN

531. Portman Road

532. Paul Jewell

533. 1981

534. Blue and White

535. Fabian Wilnis

536.   16th

537.   £3

538.   Arsenal

539.   George Burley

540.   2002 (during the 2001/2002 season)

NORWICH CITY

541.   1956

542.   Darren Huckerby

543.   Ken Brown

544.   The League Cup

545.   Grant Holt

546.   Coventry City

547.   592

548.   Flybe

549.   Ipswich Town

550.   True

WHERE DO WE PLAY - 1?

551.   Macclesfield Town

552.   Barnsley

553.   Peterborough United

554.   Bradford City

555.   Carlisle United

556.   Swindon Town

557.   Oxford United

558.   Gillingham

559.   Rochdale

560.   Chesterfield

LEEDS UNITED

561.   Ken Bates

562.   219

563.   1919

564.   True: Leeds finished 1st in 1969 and 1974, 2nd in 1965, 1966, 1970, 1971 and 1972, 3rd in 1973 and 4th in 1967 and 1968

565.   Don Revie

566.   44

567.   Peter Lorimar

568.   Elland Road

569.   Simon Grayson

570.   The FA Cup

WOLVES

571.   They are the first club to have been champions in all four divisions

572.   609

573.   Billy Wright

574.   £6.5 million each

575.   Derek Dougan

576.   2006

577.   Steve Bull

578.   The League Cup

579.   Tottenham Hotspur

580.   1877

GLENN HODDLE

581.   Wolves

582.   Chelsea

583.   Monaco (having managed Tottenham Hotspur, Swindon Town and Chelsea)

584.   1957

585.   Blackburn Rovers

586.   8

587.   Tournoi de France

588.   One

589.   Midfielder (attacking)

590.   1996

CLUB NICKNAMES

591.   Rotherham United

592.   Hereford United

593.   AFC Bournemouth

594.   Yeovil Town

595.   Lincoln City

596.   Plymouth Argyle

597.   Bristol Rovers

598.   Crewe Alexandra

599.   Walsall

600.   Bury

RAFAEL VAN DER VAART

601.   11

602.   £8 million

603.   Real Madrid

604.   Dutch

605.   True

606.   Wolves

607.   Harry Redknapp

608.   Ajax

609.   Ferdinand

610.   Sunderland

SOUTHAMPTON

611. Manchester United

612. Lawrie McMenemy

613. Mick Channon 1996-77 and 1979-82

614. Matthew Le-Tissier

615. 815

616. 49

617. The Dell

618. Nigel Adkins

619. 1885

620. Northampton Town

BOBBY ROBSON

621. Inside forward

622. PSV Eindhoven

623. Ron Greenwood

624. True

625. Twice: in 1995 and 1996

626. Fulham

627. Four

628. Ipswich Town

629. William

630. Newcastle United (between 1999 and 2004)

PREMIER LEAGUE CHAMPIONS - 2

631.	1993/1994	Manchester United
632.	1995/1996	Manchester United
633.	1997/1998	Arsenal
634.	1999/2000	Manchester United
635.	2001/2002	Arsenal
636.	2003/2004	Arsenal

637.	2005/2006	Chelsea
638.	2007/2008	Manchester United
639.	2009/2010	Chelsea
640.	2011/2012	Manchester United

DERBY COUNTY

641.	Puma
642.	The Rams
643.	1997
644.	Mart Poom
645.	1975
646.	Robbie Savage
647.	Georgi Kinkladze
648.	1884
649.	George Burley
650.	Rammie

THIERRY HENRY

651.	2007
652.	Juventus
653.	Three: in 2002, 2003 and 2005
654.	Wigan Athletic
655.	1977
656.	Middlesbrough
657.	30
658.	Monaco
659.	Daniel
660.	174

BARNSLEY

| 661. | 1997 |

662. Danny Wilson

663. The Tykes

664. 1887

665. Reuben Noble-Lazarus

666. Gerry Taggart

667. Oakwell

668. True: during the 1997/1998 season

669. Ashley Ward

670. 2009

GIANFRANCO ZOLA

671. 1996

672. West Ham United

673. 14

674. Cagliari

675. two: 1997 and 2000

676. 2004

677. False: He only never played competitive football for Chelsea in the UK

678. Ruud Gullit

679. 25

680. Parma

MERSEYSIDE DERBIES

681. Bruce Grobbelaar

682. 6-0 to Liverpool

683. 78,599

684. Gary Ablett

685. Ian Rush

686. 16

687. Dixie Dean

688.	Neville Southall

689.	Ray Clemence of Liverpool and Neville Southall of Everton

690.	They shared the FA Charity Shield after a 1-1 draw

CAPS FOR MY COUNTRY - 1

691.	Matt Holland	49 Republic of Ireland Caps, 5 goals
692.	Richard Wright	2 England Caps, 0 goals
693.	David Ginola	17 French Caps, 3 goals
694.	Dennis Bergkamp	79 Dutch Caps, 37 goals
695.	Gianfranco Zola	35 Italian Caps, 10 goals
696.	Teddy Sheringham	51 England Caps, 11 goals
697.	Tony Adams	66 England Caps, 5 goals
698.	Tony Cottee	7 England Caps, 0 goals
699.	Alan Shearer	63 England Caps, 30 goals
700.	Peter Schmeichel	129 Danish Caps, 1 goal

SHEFFIELD WEDNESDAY

701.	Sheffield United

702.	The League Cup

703.	Chris Waddle

704.	106

705.	Jack Charlton

706.	False: Kevin Pressman was sent off after just 13 seconds

707.	1867

708.	50

709.	Birmingham City

710.	2-1 AET

TONY ADAMS

711.	Wycombe Wanderers

712.	Two: 1998 and 2002 (Tony also won two First Division winners'
medals with Arsenal in 1989 and 1991)

713. Portsmouth

714. True

715. 21 (in 1988)

716. Five

717. Alexander

718. Celtic

719. 2000

720. Three: 1993, 1998 and 2002

QUEENS PARK RANGERS

721. 1882

722. Neil Warnock

723. Tottenham Hotspur

724. Clive Allen

725. Loftus Road

726. Rodney Marsh (League 30, FA Cup 3 and League Cup 11)

727. Alan McDonald

728. Newcastle United

729. 186

730. Tony Ingham

NOTTINGHAM FOREST

731. Brian Clough

732. Bob McKinlay

733. 2-2

734. £4.8 million

735. Victor Chandler

736. Stuart Pearce

737. Dave Bassett

738. 217

739. The FA Cup

740.   *Notts County*

COVENTRY CITY

741.   *1883*

742.   *2005*

743.   *Ernie Hunt*

744.   *173*

745.   *Gordon Strachan*

746.   *Sixth*

747.   *Stern John*

748.   *Steve Ogrizovic*

749.   *Tottenham Hotspur*

750.   *The Sky Blues*

THE DUTCH

751.   *Ed de Goey*   *Chelsea*

752.   *Wim Jonk*   *Sheffield Wednesday*

753.   *Clyde Wijnhard*   *Leeds United*

754.   *Bryan Roy*   *Nottingham Forest*

755.   *Jordi Cruyff*   *Manchester United*

756.   *Arnold Muhren*   *Ipswich Town*

757.   *Paul Bosvelt*   *Manchester City*

758.   *Denis Bergkamp*   *Arsenal*

759.   *Wilfred Bouma*   *Aston Villa*

760.   *Patrick Kluivert*   *Newcastle United*

STEVE BRUCE

761.   *Gillingham*

762.   *£800,000*

763.   *414(4)*

764.   *Roger*

765. Birmingham City

766. Three (1993, 1994 and 1996)

767. 1960

768. Sheffield United

769. Portsmouth

770. False: He never played for the England first squad

WHERE DO WE PLAY - 2?

771. Notts County

772. Morecambe

773. Port Vale

774. Tranmere Rovers

775. Brentford

776. Doncaster Rovers

777. Southend United

778. Oldham Athletic

779. Wycombe Wanderers

780. Leyton Orient

WALES

781. 85

782. Neville Southall

783. John Toshack

784. True: Wales lost to Brazil 1-0 in the Quarter Final

785. 28

786. Gareth Bale

787. The Millennium Stadium, Cardiff

788. The Dragons

789. France

790. Mark Hughes

LEICESTER CITY

791. Sven-Goran Eriksson

792. Adam Black

793. Matty Fryatt

794. Brian Little

795. The League Cup

796. 2002

797. The Foxes

798. Gary Lineker

799. Walkers Crisp

800. 273

GOALKEEPERS

801.	Pat Jennings	Watford
802.	Peter Shilton	Leicester City
803.	Gordon Banks	Chesterfield
804.	Neville Southall	Bury
805.	Ray Clemence	Scunthorpe United
806.	Joe Corrigan	Manchester City
807.	Peter Bonetti	Chelsea
808.	David Seaman	Peterborough United
809.	Mervyn Day	West Ham United
810.	Phil Parkes	Wolverhampton Wanderers

DENNIS BERGKAMP

811. 1995

812. Ajax

813. Three: 1998, 2002 and 2004

814. 16

815. True

816. Bruce Rioch

817. *Flying*

818. *Inter Milan*

819. *False: Dennis won four FA Cup winners' medals (in 1998, 2002, 2003 and 2005)*

820. *1998*

PLAYERS HONOURS

821.	Gary Mabbutt	FA Cup winner in 1991 (Tottenham Hotspur)
822.	Diego Forlan	Premier League winner in 2003 (Manchester United)
823.	Colin Hendry	Premier League winner in 2005 (Blackburn Rovers)
824.	Dennis Wise	FA Cup winners in 1997 and 2000 (Chelsea)
825.	Savo Milosevic	League Cup winner in 1996 (Aston Villa)
826.	Robbie Fowler	League Cup winner in 1995 and 2001 (Liverpool)
827.	Sol Campbell	League Cup winner in 1999 (Tottenham Hotspur)
828.	David James	FA Cup winner in 2008 (Portsmouth)
829.	Robbie Savage	League Cup winner in 2000 (Leicester City)
830.	Steve Bruce	FA Cup winner in 1990, 1994 and 1996 (Manchester United)

WATFORD

831. **Luther Blissett**

832. **148**

833. **Second**

834.   Graham Taylor

835.   Sir Elton John

836.   Luton Town

837.   Tony Coton

838.   Aidy Boothroyd

839.   1881

840.   Vicarage Road

DAVID O'LEARY

841.   Centre back

842.   True: He signed for Leeds United from Arsenal in 1993

843.   Aston Villa

844.   Anthony

845.   1998

846.   722

847.   Stoke Newington

848.   68

849.   The FA Cup and League Cup

850.   True: He played for Shamrock Rovers and Celtic and was capped seven times for the Republic of Ireland

GROUNDS - 2

851.   Blackburn Rovers   Ewood Park

852.   Stoke City   Britannia Stadium

853.   Queens Park Rangers   Loftus Road

854.   Manchester City   City Of Manchester Stadium

855.   West Bromwich Albion   The Hawthorns

856.   Derby County   Pride Park Stadium

857.   Everton   Goodison Park

858.   Crystal Palace   Selhurst Park

859.   Portsmouth   Fratton Park

| 860. | Oldham Athletic | Boundary Park |

HULL CITY

861. Kingston Communication Stadium

862. The Tigers

863. 2008

864. Andy Davidson

865. Roary the Tiger

866. 1904

867. Bristol City

868. Fulham

869. Boothferry Park

870. Black and amber

TEDDY SHERINGHAM

871. Colchester United

872. Three: During the 1998/99, 1999/2000 and 2000/01 seasons

873. 11

874. Millwall

875. Paul

876. Score a hat-trick (against Bolton Wanderers)

877. 31

878. 2007

879. Tottenham Hotspur

880. Striker

PORTSMOUTH

881. Cardiff City

882. Pompey

883. Southampton

884. 1949 and 1950

885.   *42*

886.   *Jimmy Dickinson*

887.   *194*

888.   *Peter Crouch*

889.   *Fratton park*

890.   *Harry Redknapp*

ROBERTO MANCINI

891.   *Inter Milan*

892.   *Leicester City*

893.   *2009*

894.   *Mark Hughes*

895.   *December*

896.   *Fifth (2009/2010 season)*

897.   *True: Fifth (2009/2010 season)*

898.   *Stoke City (December 2009)*

899.   *Italian*

900.   *1997 (The Italian Player of the Year award)*

NORTHERN IRELAND

901.   *Pat Jennings 1964-86*

902.   *Windsor Park, Belfast*

903.   *12 (1990-2000)*

904.   *Billy Bingham*

905.   *The Green and White Army*

906.   *True*

907.   *Gerry Armstrong*

908.   *David Healy*

909.   *1-0 with David Healy scoring in the 73rd minute*

910.   *Nigel Worthington*

CLUB NICKNAMES - 2

911. Wycombe Wanderers

912. Northampton Town

913. Exeter City

914. Leyton Orient

915. Brighton & Hove Albion

916. Shrewsbury Town

917. Huddersfield Town

918. Port Vale

919. Morecambe

920. Torquay United

RUUD GULLIT

921. Dutch

922. FA Cup winner in 1997

923. True (FA Cup in 1997)

924. Four

925. True

926. Newcastle United

927. True

928. AC Milan

929. Glenn Hoddle

930. Feyenoord

CRYSTAL PALACE

931. The Glaziers

932. 660

933. Danny Butterfield

934. Andrew Johnson

935. Terry Vanables

936. 153

937. Andrew Johnson

938. Manchester United

939. 1905

940. Sheffield Wednesday

MIDFIELDERS

941.	Bryan Robson	Middlesbrough
942.	Liam Brady	West Ham United
943.	Graeme Souness	Rangers
944.	Glenn Hoddle	Chelsea
945.	Johnny Haynes	Maritzburg
946.	Ray Wilkins	Leyton Orient
947.	Colin Bell	San Jose Earthquakes
948.	Danny Blanchflower	Tottenham Hotspur
949.	Willie Carr	Stourbridge
950.	Billy Bremner	Doncaster Rovers

IAN WRIGHT

951. Crystal Palace 206(19) = 225 and Arsenal 212(9) = 221

952. 33

953. Burnley

954. 128

955. West Ham United

956. Edward

957. £2.5 million

958. Graham Taylor

959. MBE

960. Millwall

TEAM NICKNAMES – 2

| 961. | Leicester City | The Foxes |

962.	West Bromwich Albion	The Baggies
963.	Southampton	The Saints
964.	Liverpool	The Reds
965.	Reading	The Royals
966.	Coventry City	The Sky Blues
967.	Fulham	The Cottagers
968.	Wigan Athletic	The Latics
969.	Ipswich Town	The Blues
970.	Bolton Wanderers	The Trotters

DIDIER DROGBA

971. 11

972. Marseille

973. Ivory Coast

974. Centre forward

975. £24 million

976. West Bromwich Albion

977. 1978

978. Wigan Athletic

979. 10

980. Frank Lampard

SHEFFIELD UNITED

981. The Blades

982. True

983. Four: in 1899, 1902, 1915 and 1925

984. Neil Warnock

985. 1982 (1981/1982 season)

986. James Beattie

987. Joe Shaw

988. Dave Bassett

989.   *HFS Loans*

990.   *1899*

CAPS FOR MY COUNTRY – 2

991.	David Seaman	75 England Caps, 0 goals
992.	Anders Limpar	58 Swedish Caps, goals
993.	Ally McCoist	61 Scottish Caps, 19 goals
994.	Efan Ekoku	20 Nigerian Caps, 6 goals
995.	Marcel Desailly	116 French Caps, 3 goals
996.	Paul Gascoigne	57 England Caps, 10 goals
997.	Frank Leboeuf	50 French Caps, 5 goals
998.	Sol Campbell	73 England Caps, 1 goal
999.	Gianluca Vialli	59 Italian Caps, 16 goals
1000.	Des Walker	59 England Caps, 0 goals

NOTES:

NOTES:

NOTES:

NOTES:

NOTES:

NOTES:

OTHER BOOKS BY CHRIS COWLIN:

* Celebrities' Favourite Football Teams

* The British TV Sitcom Quiz Book

* The Cricket Quiz Book

* The Gooners Quiz Book

* The Horror Film Quiz Book

* The Official Aston Villa Quiz Book

* The Official Birmingham City Quiz Book

* The Official Brentford Quiz Book

* The Official Bristol Rovers Quiz Book

* The Official Burnley Quiz Book

* The Official Bury Quiz Book

* The Official Carlisle United Quiz Book

* The Official Carry On Quiz Book

* The Official Chesterfield Football Club Quiz Book

* The Official Colchester United Quiz Book

* The Official Coventry City Quiz Book

* The Official Doncaster Rovers Quiz Book

* The Official Greenock Morton Quiz Book

* The Official Heart of Midlothian Quiz Book

* The Official Hereford United Quiz Book

* The Official Hull City Quiz Book

* The Official Ipswich Town Quiz Book

OTHER BOOKS BY CHRIS COWLIN:

* The Official Leicester City Quiz Book

* The Official Macclesfield Town Quiz Book

* The Official Norwich City Football Club Quiz

* The Official Notts County Quiz Book

* The Official Peterborough United Quiz Book

* The Official Port Vale Quiz Book

* The Official Queen of the South Quiz Book

* The Official Rochdale AFC Quiz Book

* The Official Rotherham United Quiz Book

* The Official Sheffield United Quiz Book

* The Official Shrewsbury Town Quiz Book

* The Official Stockport County Quiz Book

* The Official Walsall Football Club Quiz Book

* The Official Watford Football Club Quiz Book

* The Official West Bromwich Albion Quiz Book

* The Official Wolves Quiz Book

* The Official Yeovil Town Quiz Book

* The Reality Television Quiz Book

* The Southend United Quiz Book

* The Spurs Quiz Book

* The Sunderland AFC Quiz Book

* The Ultimate Derby County Quiz Book

* The West Ham United Quiz Book

www.apexpublishing.co.uk